SLOW
THEOLOGY

"This book is a breath of fresh air—humble and thoughtful but full of conviction that the way of Jesus is worth pursuing. *Slow Theology* does not merely affirm important theological conclusions, it articulates a way of thinking—and living—theologically. Whether you are skeptical about Christianity or exhausted with theological bickering, A. J. and Nijay present a vision of Christian theology that just might inspire you to greater study of and relationship with God."

—**Kaitlyn Schiess**, senior editor, Holy Post Media; author
of *The Ballot and the Bible: How Scripture Has Been Used
and Abused in American Politics and Where We Go from Here*

"Swoboda and Gupta offer us a way to do theology that is slow in a 24/7 world, focused in a distracted age, thoughtful in judgmental places, and contemplative instead of taking the clickbait. They urge us to find rest in Christ from our worries and labors. A great invitation to slow down, breathe, and believe afresh."

—**Michael F. Bird**, deputy principal, Ridley College,
Melbourne, Australia

"This book reminded me that sometimes we will get to where we are going quicker if we are willing to slow down. A. J. and Nijay are calm voices of leadership in a time of great chaos. *Slow Theology* will help you endure."

—**Heather Thompson Day**, author of *What If I'm Wrong?*

"T. S. Eliot once asked, 'Where is the life we have lost in living?' Today, many are asking the same question. We are living at a pace that is unsustainable, doing violence to our souls. In *Slow Theology*, A. J. Swoboda and Nijay Gupta paint a beautiful, compelling, and deeply theological vision of living and walking with God at a pace that humanizes, nourishes, and leads to the flourishing of our souls."

—**Jon Tyson**, author and pastor of Church of the City
New York (jontyson.org)

"Ours is an age that prizes quick takes, sharp certainties, and tidy solutions. But faith doesn't rush. *Slow Theology* invites us to pause—really pause—to dwell with God in the questions, to make peace with mystery, and to journey through the rugged terrain of belief with resilience and hope. A. J. Swoboda and Nijay Gupta offer not only profound theological insight but also pastoral wisdom shaped by suffering, beauty, and a trust in the slow, redemptive work of God. This book does not shy away from the chaos of our time; instead, it dares to suggest that chaos might be the very compost from which Christlikeness can grow. Every page pulses with grace, truth, and an unflinching belief in the God who never rushes but always redeems. I will be recommending this book to pastors, students, and weary saints everywhere."

—**Tara Beth Leach**, author of *The Great Morning Revolution*

SLOW
THEOLOGY

Eight Practices for Resilient Faith
in a Turbulent World

A. J. SWOBODA AND
NIJAY K. GUPTA

 BrazosPress
a division of Baker Publishing Group
Grand Rapids, Michigan

Published by Brazos Press
a division of Baker Publishing Group
Grand Rapids, Michigan
BrazosPress.com

Printed in the United States of America

Library of Congress Cataloging-in-Publication Data
Names: Swoboda, A. J., 1981– author | Gupta, Nijay K. author
Title: Slow theology : eight practices for resilient faith in a turbulent world / A. J.
   Swoboda and Nijay K. Gupta.
Description: Grand Rapids, Michigan : Brazos Press, a division of Baker
   Publishing Group, [2025] | Includes bibliographical references.
Identifiers: LCCN 2025007700 | ISBN 9781587436437 paperback | ISBN
   9781587436857 casebound | ISBN 9781493452170 ebook
Subjects: LCSH: Resilience (Personality trait)—Religious aspects—Christianity |
   Trust in God—Christianity
Classification: LCC BV4597.58.R47 S963 2025 | DDC 233/.5—dc23/eng/20250527
LC record available at https://lccn.loc.gov/2025007700

Cover design by Studio Gearbox

Baker Publishing Group publications use paper produced from sustainable forestry
practices and postconsumer waste whenever possible.

25 26 27 28 29 30 31   7 6 5 4 3 2 1

Live slowly enough to be able to think deeply about God.

—J. I. Packer

CONTENTS

FOREWORD

The farmers in the old prairie days used to prepare for a winter storm by putting up a rope between the house and the barn. They did this because they knew that in a swirling blizzard, even a brief distance, such as the walk from their house to the barn, could be confusing and disorienting. That familiar journey they had taken hundreds of times could become a strange terrain, leaving them to freeze in the cold winter night. But with the rope, they knew they could always find their way home.

We live in a confusing cultural moment. Opinions about God and what it means to be a Christian swirl all around us. Conflicting voices compete for our attention. To add to the storm, Christianity has been corrupted and co-opted by cultural forces and personal agendas. We've witnessed church leaders fail and fall and cause great harm. Maybe all of that has left you wanting to walk away. At the very least, you're wondering where you belong. You find yourself being haunted with a kind of spiritual homelessness. The church has lost its way, and now so have you. We need a rope in the blizzard, something to lead us home to the heart of our faith.

I've come to see the Nicene Creed as the rope that has served the church for 1,700 years. This instrument of unity reminds us of what binds us together as followers of Jesus. Christians are prone to argue and divide over many things, some that matter greatly and some that don't. Throughout church history, the creed has served as a confessional reminder that the things that *define* us as Christians ought to *unite* us as Christians. In that way, the creed is not just an instrument of unity; it is also a guide in uncertainty, a path in the wild reminding us of the faith of the apostles. After all, it was drafted at a time when false teachers were gaining traction and popularity, threatening to corrupt the church.

The creed gives us an outline of doctrine. It is meant as a resource for worship. That is how it is used in churches all around the world today. As someone who led worship for many years in the church, I recognize that the creed is structured similar to a hymn—organized in stanzas around the Father, Son, and Holy Spirit. Confessed in faith with the community of God's people in the gathering of worship, these words become an invitation into the glorious mystery of knowing the Father, Son, and Holy Spirit.

I have written about all this, and yet I know there's something missing. The creed is not enough. The creed gives us *the* faith—its content and perhaps more accurately its object, the triune God himself. But there is still work to be done to cultivate *our* faith—the act of believing. If the creed is the rope, our confession of it is the grip. This is where things start to get precarious. Faith in this sense can feel like a different kind of rope—a tightrope. And we are trying to walk across. Make one error, and you plunge to disaster on either side. You could fall due to believing the wrong thing, or you could fall due to believing the right thing too rigidly or too loosely. Dangers lurk all around.

We feel these perils acutely because we have been conditioned to think of faith as something we must hold to on our own. If we cannot verify and validate each claim ourselves, our faith is at risk. There are many ways to explain the roots of our spiritual paranoia. Perhaps it comes from our American individualism. Maybe it's the unintended consequence of an emphasis on a personal faith.

We've taken "personal" to mean individual or even private. Or maybe it's the fixation on a particular kind of knowledge—the kind that comes from proofs and probabilities and results in certainty. Whatever the case, our ability to believe has become a tightrope that we must be careful not to fall from.

"We Believe In . . ."

Look again at the creed. There are three clues from the early church. In many modern versions, the repeated opening words of each stanza are "We believe in . . ." "We" because faith is never a solo act. We are always in the company of the church—when we pray, when we worship, when we confess our faith. We are joined by the billions of Christians alive on the earth right now and by the billions more who have gone before. Faith is not precarious, because it does not depend on us. When our faith is weak, someone else's is strong. We are carried by the great company of the saints, of all who believe in Jesus. Faith is a community project.

Faith is not like a one-person kayak or the stand-up paddleboards I see in the Back Bay at Newport Beach. If we think of faith that way, then when we struggle to row the oars of faith—as we inevitably will—we will conclude that we should get out of the boat. But faith for the Christian is much more like an old galley ship from the Roman era where hundreds of people row to keep it moving. If one person were to stop rowing, the boat would still keep moving. The Christian faith did not begin with us, and it is not up to us to keep it going.

It's helpful to remind ourselves that we belong to the global church and the historic church—a story and a family that goes back two thousand years and spans the globe. We are not the center. If you're struggling with faith and need to set down your oar for a season, that's fine. Just stay in the boat. Don't jump overboard. Faith is not a solo sport. Let others row when you cannot. This book is a way of staying in the boat.

Then there is the second clue from the creed, the word "believe." Belief is not certainty. It is conviction, but it is *humble* conviction. It requires a bowing of the head to a mystery beyond us. Every encounter with the divine given to us in the Bible involves people falling down—falling to their knees, falling on their faces. Certainty breeds arrogance. It allows us to be puffed up with knowledge. But true faith is gentle and humble. It lowers us. It leads us to confess our smallness in the face of God's largeness.

Yet belief is not fragile. Faith gets stronger through testing. Over and over, the Bible shows us women and men who are allowed and even led into places of great testing. The testing is not to provide an answer to God, as though he did not know the quality of their faith. The testing is for the benefit of the believer. It is intended to bring us through the fire with a stronger faith.

In my work on pastoral resilience, I have found it helpful to define "resilience" in two ways. First, it is a kind of return or *recovery*. One of the markers of health is the rate of recovery. In a stress test, the doctor pushes you to an elevated heart rate—to let you experience stress and duress—and then evaluates how quickly you return to a resting heart rate. Odds are, you will experience the testing of your faith in this life. Jesus just about assured us of it: "In this world you will have trouble" (John 16:33). You are not a bad Christian because you experience doubt. The key is in how you are able to return to a place of rest and trust in Christ. The second aspect of resilience is *recalibration*. We don't just recover from a turbulent test of faith; we retool and rebuild; we reinforce and realign. The goal, as this book attests, is to get stronger, to become antifragile.

Now we come to the third and final clue from the creed: the word "in." Believing *in* is different from believing *that*. The best illustration of the difference is a story about a tightrope. French acrobat Charles Blondin walked across Niagara Falls on a tightrope a number of times. There's a legend that after a few trips, he decided to ask for a volunteer to ride on his back. No one stepped forward. "Believing *that*" something is true is like saying, "Yes! Blondin! We believe that you can do this!" But "believing *in*" is actually getting on his back.

This next part of the story is true, with pictures to prove it. Blondin's manager, Harry Colcord, rode on Blondin's back as Blondin walked across a tightrope over the falls. Blondin told his manager as they began, "Look up, Harry. . . . You are no longer Colcord, you are Blondin. Until I clear this place be a part of me, mind, body, and soul. If I sway, sway with me. Do not attempt to do any balancing yourself. If you do, we will both go to our death."[1]

It sounds quite a bit like Paul's own summation of his spiritual formation: "I have been crucified with Christ and I no longer live, but Christ lives in me. The life I now live in the body, I live by faith in the Son of God, who loved me and gave himself for me" (Gal. 2:20).

Faith is more than cheering from the banks of the falls. Faith is not simply believing *that* there is a God; it is drawing near to God. Yes, the creed is our rope back home. But if faith is also like a tightrope, then all along the walk, we must cling to Jesus above all. That kind of proximity to Jesus is where this book will lead you.

Faith and Faithfulness

Nijay and A. J. have given us an extraordinary book about faith. By that I mean not only the content of our faith—they are experts on that topic too—but much more the nature of our faith. It's about how to cultivate faith that lasts. This is a book about *faithfulness*—holding fast to faith until the end, when faith becomes sight and all things are made new.

With the nuance and insight of professors and the tender touch of pastors, they write profoundly and personally. They offer practices to form you and stories to move you. Best of all, they are writing not merely from concepts they've learned; this is wisdom that has come through their lives to you. The testing of our faith—through doubt, suffering, and more—refines it and makes it stronger. It has been true for them, and it can be true for you.

Through it all, you will feel the community of faith carrying you. You will have been led into the slowed-down awe of belief. And you will find your heart firmly fixed on the Faithful One, Christ himself. In the end, it is not we who are holding on to him but he who is holding on to us.

Glenn Packiam
lead pastor, Rockharbor Church;
author of *What's a Christian, Anyway?*
and *The Resilient Pastor*

INTRODUCTION

Good Poison

We begin with World War II. On December 2, 1943, a German air raid in Italy sank over a dozen ships docked in port. Among them was an American vessel carrying over two thousand mustard gas bombs intended for the war. Soon, toxic gas began leaking from the SS *John Harvey* into the air and water. At the same time, servicemen—desperate to save themselves—jumped overboard, attempting to swim to safety. Tragically, this placed them in direct contact with the contaminated waters. Unaware of the danger, the soldiers were submerged in the poisonous water surrounding the sinking ship. Hundreds of American sailors were exposed to the toxin, suffering severe injuries. Nearly a hundred men lost their lives.

Thankfully, not all were lost. In the aftermath of the disaster, doctors sought to treat those who'd survived the horrific conditions as best they could. However, in the course of doing so, they discovered something startling. Though the surviving men had been heavily exposed to the mustard gas, they appeared to exhibit a perplexing change in the way their blood cells functioned. The gas's destructive effects appeared to prevent the white blood cells from replicating—the very cells that would have helped the body heal. This was undoubtedly a terrible wartime tragedy. But this tragedy soon led to a discovery that would change medical science. Sparked by curiosity, researchers began wondering if the mustard gas could actually be redesigned to heal. Could this poison *also* shrink tumors and kill cancer cells?

A major breakthrough would soon come. Five years later, scientists developed an experimental treatment called Mustargen (mechlorethamine). Today, we know this chemical by its more popular name: chemotherapy. For the first time, a seemingly effective chemical therapy was made publicly available to treat cancer. Since this breakthrough, countless therapies have been developed and millions of lives have been saved. It's astonishing to think that the tens of millions of people who have undergone chemotherapy for cancer treatment over the past seventy-five years owe it all to the deadly effects of mustard gas. Some poisons, it seems, have the power to kill *and* the power to heal.

Mustargen offers us a powerful lesson about the very nature of the Christian story—namely, that the things in life that appear to be momentary tragedies can be turned into tremendous goods. In the right hands, any tragedy can become a comedy. Which is good news given what we find in the Bible. The late, great Christian writer Frederick Buechner gives honest reflection to the dark, difficult storyline of the Bible:

> [The Bible] is a swarming compost of a book, an Irish stew of poetry and propaganda, law and legalism, myth and murk, history and hysteria. Over the centuries it has become hopelessly associated with tub-thumping evangelism and dreary piety, with superannuated superstition and blue-nosed moralizing, with ecclesiastical authoritarianism and crippling literalism. . . . And yet—and yet—just because it is a book about both the sublime and the unspeakable, it is a book also about life the way it really is. It is a book about people who at one and the same time can be both believing and unbelieving, innocent and guilty, crusaders and crooks, full of hope and full of despair. In other words, it is a book about us.[1]

Indeed, the Bible is a book that deals with great pain. And it is a book that has been wrongly used and manipulated to undertake many evils. For Buechner, though, and any reader of the *whole* Bible, what may appear to be a tale of endless tragedy, heartbreak, and trauma is a good story. The resounding message of this sacred account is that despite every last pain and setback in the story of creation, the God of the Bible refuses to give up on what he has made. Indeed, one could sum up the story of the entire Bible as a paraphrase of Genesis 50:20—what was intended for evil, God has masterfully turned into good.

To be a follower of the way of Jesus is to embrace this hope that God will eventually turn all evil and darkness into good and light on the day of his glorious restoration. We all look and long for that day. But what if followers of Jesus aren't meant to simply wait until that future event to learn from, be formed by, and be renewed by the painful stories of our lives? What if all those difficulties and setbacks could actually make us stronger, deeper, and more resilient *today*?

Poison, in some instances, can actually save a life. It's no wonder chemotherapy has been nicknamed "good poison." However, every cancer patient knows that chemotherapy is beneficial only in precise dosages. The very chemical that can save a life was originally designed to kill in the context of war. Every medical practitioner, at some point in their education, learns the ancient wisdom of Paracelsus (1493–1541): "Everything is poison, there is poison in everything. Only the dose makes a thing not a poison."[2]

What if it is only out of the "swarming compost" of our lives that the fruit of Christlikeness can grow?

The Gift of the Chaos

We live in chaotic times. While the church has endured countless difficult eras in her long and storied history, the modern moment feels uniquely unmoored and out of control. So many things seem to be off-kilter: Social trust in institutions continues to erode, marriages and families are falling apart, the economy is topsy-turvy at best, politics has become violently tribal, suicide rates are rising, and many are reconsidering (and recanting) their commitments to the Christian faith. No one would deny that these are hard times. But are they worse than previous moments in history? Indeed, they are not. Rather, they *feel* as though they are uniquely unparalleled and chaotic. There just seem to be so many new problems and crises—and fewer and fewer solutions for dealing with them.

The present emotional tumult is similar to a phenomenon we observe every single fall on our university campuses. Just before classes begin in September, we get our first sight of a whole new class of first-year students as they descend on the university for the first time. As soon as their parents leave, these emerging adults begin to discover a whole new world. While they may have come to college with a deep love for Jesus, the church, and the Bible, they quickly find themselves in a world of new questions, realities, and complexities they didn't even know existed just a few short weeks prior. This chaotic experience can be overwhelming. Some move home after the first term. But most stay—and embrace the difficult journey before them as part of their education.

These students entering this new world may feel as though they are doing something that nobody else has ever done. But the reality is, this is not a new experience. Rather, it is a new experience *for them*. As we enter what feels like a new world, we would be wise to recognize that there is nothing new about it. It is just new to us. For sure, the church has entered a new time and a new place. And the experience is enduringly disruptive. But this is nothing new for the church. It is merely new *to us*.

The reality remains that (historically speaking) nothing is new about our moment in time. Christians of every culture, denomination, and generation seem to face a whole new litany of theological, cultural, and relational challenges. But we mustn't forget: "There is nothing new under the sun" (Eccles. 1:9). History mustn't be forgotten. God's people have endured moments like these before. Lord knows, the church has survived multiple world wars, countless scandals, plagues, and pandemics, yet still it stands. We're just far more *hyper*aware of the challenges we face because they are happening on our watch, in real time, and on the screens in our pockets. The church, like an undergraduate student, has entered a world that feels so new. But the question remains: Will they pack their bags and go home? Or stay as part of their education? Staying requires boldness, courage, and resilience—for we cannot choose the time in which we live. All we can choose is whether to be faithful with the time in which we have been placed. In the wisdom of Gandalf to Frodo in J. R. R. Tolkien's classic, *The Fellowship of the Ring*: "So do all who live to see such times. But that is not for them to decide. All you have to decide is what to do with the time that is given to you."[3]

Christians can tend to respond to the difficulties of the culture and time by building a moat or fence to protect themselves from the onslaught of the world. This may seem reasonable, even prudent. But by walling themselves off—severing relationships with those who think differently—they not only are unable to hear the voice of a hurt and wounded world; they also cut off the possibility of being heard. These silos may feel safe and protected, but they remove us from God's call to be in the world to love it into the arms of Christ. This isn't God's way.

When we look at the garden of Eden, we find that God contented himself in creating a space where a serpent is permitted to roam freely with the power to speak, question, and deceive. Apparently, God did not create a garden with a moat, wall, or silo. Nor does God, in suffering the pain of humanity's choice to listen to the serpent's deception, wall himself off in heaven to protect himself from the pain of heartache. No. In a world of deception, lies, and chaos, the very heart of God is to seek and save those who are lost. He creates a good garden where pain is a possibility. And he restores it by *leaving* heaven to come to a broken and hurting world.

God has entrusted us to swim the choppy, uncertain, terrifying waters of the present. We didn't choose this. Nor can we get out of it. Our response is all we can choose. To do so well, we must be willing to consider a strange and seemingly uncomfortable question: What if this chaos we are experiencing can actually strengthen us? What if it is something intended by God to make us stronger? What if what we've assumed is a crisis is actually just God's way of growing us up?

Just as new students entering college are immersed in questions that are new to them, so are many people in the church. Is God good? Why is the Bible to be trusted? Is Christianity toxic or life-giving? This onslaught of questions has led to what many people have called the "deconstruction" experience.[4] There is no shared definition of what this experience means. For some, it means the reconsideration and rethinking of faith so that it may be strengthened. For others, however, deconstruction is more akin to deconversion—leaving the faith altogether. Sadly, far too many fail to recognize the power and healing that comes from being able to walk through the experience of scrutinizing what one believes in the hopes of coming out the other side with a deeper and more vital faith.

This is why the image of chemotherapy is apt for this phenomenon and this time in history. There is great power in asking serious questions about one's faith and scrutinizing the genuineness and morality of Christians of the past and present. This can be crucial for rooting out and discarding things that are not conducive to knowing and following Jesus. Deconstruction, at its best, can be undertaken to break down and remove bad theology and address trauma experienced in the church firsthand or secondhand. In this sense, it is like "good poison." But if we spend all or most of our time with the cynical Christian or bitter ex-Christian, it can easily become toxic to our faith. Heed Paracelsus's warning: Make sure to get the dosage right. Deconstruction in the proper dose can save one's faith, but the wrong dose can be fatal.

For those who begin to recognize the false ways that they have been handed the Christian faith, deconstruction can be the very means by which the toxicity of bad theology is cut away from genuine faith. A natural part of maturity *should* be to reassess and reevaluate one's faith to ensure that what has been given is indeed faithful to the Jesus Christ who is revealed in Scripture.

Still, God has created a good world that is permitted to contain dangerous voices. God's garden had no moat. We have taken advantage of our freedom to rebel. We live in a world where the serpent is permitted to slither around and challenge the faithful. All this reminds us that faith in God is hard work. Jesus told his disciples that this is the essence of true humanity: "The work of God is this: to believe in the one he has sent" (John 6:29). The work of God in our lives is to believe, trust, and cultivate love toward God. But it should be clearly stated that this is work. It requires our full attention, our deep devotion, and our unflinching commitment to finishing the race.

The Purpose of This Book

This book seeks to offer our readers eight biblically and theologically informed practices for how they can develop a faith that withstands the many challenges of the present world. Our conviction is that these challenges we face can, if walked carefully, make us deeper followers of Jesus. In his 2014 book *Antifragile*, social theorist and philosopher Nassim Taleb tackles what he notes are epic changes in culture—particularly in the Western world.[5] He argues that most people have not been prepared for the changes we currently face. Much of the Western world has fostered an environment that uniquely forms fragile people and institutions who cannot handle change or rapid variability. Taleb's basic premise is that tremendous benefits come from being challenged intellectually and socially, and that people in the West must learn to become antifragile.

This concept of antifragility speaks to so many of the challenges that the church of the twenty-first century is facing. Questions and concerns are being raised at a level that is nearly impossible to keep up with: changes in social orders, nations rising and falling, political chaos, evolving views of sexuality and gender, the rise of artificial intelligence. The list could go on. And it will go on. As technological advances continue, the changes will continue to proliferate at a breakneck speed.

What if God's people slowed down and put careful thought, attention, and discipline into cultivating antifragility? What would that look like? An *antifragile* Christian church

- would be secure in and focus more on the words of Christ than on its standing in the world
- would be able to hear from God even when it is being screamed at by the world
- would not allow the chaos of the world to rob it of its peace
- would remain faithful to its calling as the culture constantly shifts what it believes
- would be more committed to going where God desires it to go than where the world would want it to go

These are tall orders but utterly necessary. It is important to note that, for Taleb, the idea of *antifragility* entails so much more than merely enduring chaos. We don't need mere endurance. We need something so much more than that. Being antifragile goes far beyond simply enduring; we actually become stronger and *improve* as we face difficulty. To endure, writes Taleb, is to "resist shocks and stay the same. . . . The antifragile gets better."[6] Exposure to chaos can actually make us stronger when we face it well. Just as a tree depends on wind to grow its roots down deep, so too we need great difficulty to be able to go deeper into the life of Jesus Christ.

To be sure, Taleb never applies his concept of antifragility to the realm of church, theology, or discipleship. Nevertheless, the concept is invaluable and instructive for Christians in today's world. The church has always been challenged to answer Christ's call to persevere—a theme that is woven throughout the biblical narrative (see, e.g., Rom. 5:3–4; Gal. 6:9; James 1:12). Christians who have been sent into the world as salt and light are called by God to withstand and flourish amid the onslaught of cultural changes. They are called not to wither but to grow.

And that is exactly what the early church did. In its first three hundred years, when it was the most persecuted, marginalized, and oppressed, the church exploded with growth, depth, and power. It was *as* they were killed that they most walked in the power of Jesus. And the numbers back this up. Some scholars have estimated that in AD 100 there were approximately twenty-five thousand followers of Jesus. By the year 310, there were believed to be about thirty million Christians.[7] All at a time when the church was most marginalized and silenced by the Roman Empire. Indeed, in the book of Acts, every time the church is displaced due to these forces, it always ends up growing. Displacement was just God's way of planting new trees.

The church of Jesus Christ is called to be the most antifragile community on the planet. What can we do to develop a faith that not only is resilient through difficulty but actually grows as it faces challenges? What if, by God's grace, every new question we asked was not a problem? What if it was just a way for our faith to become deeper?

Throughout this book, we will offer what we believe are eight distinct ways to slow down, listen patiently to God, and cultivate an antifragile faith:

- Take your time—learn to make slow, meditative, and incessantly thoughtful decisions based on prayer, community, and intentionality.

- Embrace the theological journey—see the journey of following Jesus as a lifelong struggle that won't be finished quickly.
- Think slowly—build more silence, meditation, and introspection into how we think about God and ourselves.
- Ponder the mysteries—let the difficult questions remain and don't strive to iron them out to make things easier.
- Go to the problems—don't run away from the hard stuff but run toward it.
- Let pain be the altar—allow the pains and difficulties of existence to be the thing on which we build our conversations with God.
- Believe together—see the journey of faith formation as a communal activity that is a part of one's individual discipleship pathway.
- Don't ever give up—in short, practice long-suffering and perseverance.

We write this recognizing that our readers will be diverse. Some readers of this book may have recently begun to spend a considerable amount of time reflecting on their Christian upbringing and faith. They may be questioning some of the things they were handed in their earlier faith. Some have deconstructed a lot, others less so. But if you've picked up this book, chances are you're holding on to hope for healing for your soul. Perhaps you've had to rid yourself of "harmful theology cells," but to stay alive, you need to stop consuming poison, rebuild your strength, and get healthy.

Others may have walked away from the Christian faith recently, or perhaps it happened some time ago. Maybe you drifted away, or maybe there was a traumatic event. Whatever the case, we grieve for the pain you've experienced. Picking up this book might be driven by a feeling inside you that there's still something in the

Christian faith that inspires you—that you still feel drawn to Jesus, the man of the cross, and that you have powerful memories of hope and joy from your early faith. This book could be a step in a cautious journey of beginning to walk with Jesus again. You might find inspiration from an unexpected source, a saying popular among video gamers: "I don't quit; I restart." Jesus doesn't mind a "restart." As long as there is breath in your lungs and blood in your veins, Jesus welcomes do-overs.

Let this book be an invitation to a fresh start.

The Struggle That Leads to Beauty

Jean-Dominique Bauby was widely esteemed as one of France's most prolific and influential journalists. His work widely shaped the quickly evolving cultural landscape of Europe during the 1980s and '90s. On December 8, 1995, having just signed a contract to write his next book, Bauby suffered a massive stroke that left him entirely paralyzed with a condition known as locked-in syndrome. His legs, hands, arms, and fingers were rendered entirely unmovable. The traumatic experience left the brilliant journalist, writer, and thought leader with the ability to use only one part of his entire body: his left eye.

While Bauby's body was rendered unmovable, his mind was as sharp as ever. Could he continue with his next book? Bauby soon undertook one of the most daring writing ventures known to literary history. Working alongside his speech therapist—a woman named Sandrine Fichou—Bauby found a way to develop a system to slowly blink the letters he wished to be written down. Over two whole months, working nearly three hours a day each day of the week, Bauby blinked an entire 130-page manuscript into existence. The book would eventually be called *The Diving Bell and the Butterfly*.[8] The volume offers some of the most illuminating and insightful thoughts about human existence through the lens of Bauby's experience of being able to think clearly while being unable to move. Tragically, Bauby died of pneumonia two days after the publication of his book.

Bauby's boldness illuminates for us a seemingly exotic side to life—the existence of slowing down. By narrating the inner life of someone who literally was slowed down to stillness, he invited his overworked, overscheduled, overly busy Western reader to consider what life may look like for the person who must stay still—and that life will eventually slow down for all of us to the speed of death.

People who have been forced to slow down often give us the greatest gifts. In June 2024, I (A. J.) had the opportunity to visit the Oregon State Correctional Institution in Salem, Oregon, to meet with a group of inmates who had read one of my recent books. The experience was admittedly terrifying—yet simultaneously sacred. Never before had I taken seriously Jesus's words about visiting those in prison. Sitting with a group of men who had done the unthinkable—rape, murder, violent theft—and talking about Jesus was a sobering and eye-opening experience. I was struck by the grace of Christ I saw in the eyes of many of these inmates.

As we sat in a small, well-lit classroom in the prison, the students were given permission to ask their visiting theologian any question they had. Slowly but surely, we began a nearly two-hour dialogue about all things theology, ranging from who Jesus was to why the Bible should be trusted to the existence of extraterrestrials. The room was electric. Perhaps more electric than I'd ever experienced. These men sat with full attention, present hearts, and a hungry desire to understand God and his kingdom.

As I drove home, I realized something. I'd never been in a room in which people displayed such rapt attention. Never had I seen such engaging theological dialogue and passion. Then it dawned on me. These men collectively possessed one shared experience that few in the outside world had: freedom from smartphones. These men literally had nowhere to go. Life had entirely slowed down—in many cases, for life. And the space gave them the unique quality of being present, of longing for truth, and of desiring to dialogue with their fellow prisoners.

What did Bauby and these prisoners have in common? The brilliance of David in Psalm 23 cannot be missed, nor should its details be overlooked. David, in writing about God, reflects:

> The LORD is my shepherd, I lack nothing.
> He *makes me lie down* in green pastures,
> he leads me beside quiet waters,
> he refreshes my soul. (vv. 1–3)

Keeping in mind what David constantly faced—attacks, mobs of angered citizens, and kings seeking his life—he intimately knew the experience of what he had recorded in this psalm. David, like Bauby and the prisoners, did not just experience slowing down. They were *made* to lie down.

What is most incredible about the majority of the psalms we read in the Bible is that almost all of them were written as their authors were experiencing profound chaos, enduring disruption, and, in many cases, running for their lives. Yet out of that difficulty and pain came the psalms themselves. When we read the stories of people such as Bauby, we must remember what their pain did to them. It did not stop them. It *awakened* them. The same with David. As he is writing Psalm 23, he is on the run—for his life. Only then is he awakened to write a song that we sing in church, pray often, and even imprint on bathmats.

As we begin to cultivate a slow theology and an antifragile faith, we will find that the painful realities we face soon become the fuel for our love for God.

Antifragile Faith as Building Wisely

Building an antifragile faith takes time. It can't be rushed. Consider this: It takes (on average) around twelve to eighteen months to construct a new single-family home in America. This process includes laying the foundation, framing, exterior and interior work, and final touches. However, in 2005, a construction company made headlines by completing the fastest home build ever. On October 1, they constructed a 2,249 square foot house in just 2 hours, 52 minutes, and 29 seconds. Known as the Two-Hour House, this impressive feat involved a team of eight hundred volunteers. (Rumor has it the house is still standing, and you can visit it in Tyler, Texas.) While this makes for a great story and demonstrates what a team can achieve under pressure, there are countless examples of buildings that have fallen apart due to rushed construction.

One of the most famous incidents is the collapse of the Sampoong Department Store in Seoul, South Korea, in 1995. Builder Lee Joon originally conceived of this endeavor as a four-story apartment complex but changed his mind and wanted to convert it for commercial use after the work had already begun. His push for speedy construction meant the building went up in about three years, when such a massive project should have taken at least twice as long. That meant Joon cut many corners, including providing insufficient support columns and not properly accommodating for the weight of machinery in the building. Whenever advisers and contractors questioned his choices, he fired them and hired whoever would follow his instructions. About five years after the store opened, large cracks in the structure were noticeable and brought to Joon's attention. He called his workers to find solutions, but he refused to evacuate the shoppers—although he did request certain executives move to safety. When the building finally collapsed, five hundred people were killed and more than nine hundred were injured. This was the largest loss of life in a building collapse in modern history until the events of 9/11.

Jesus had something to say about how to build a house well. Near the end of what we call the Sermon on the Mount, he invited his disciples to consider how they should build their own lives. A life built wisely and well is designed to withstand harsh conditions like flooding and heavy winds. The wise person follows Jesus closely and listens to him and only him. But the foolish person doesn't lay a solid foundation and is unprepared for harsh conditions, and their life and faith can be ruined all too easily.

But what happens when you ignorantly build your *life* on a weak foundation—leaning too much on a certain pastor or author or church or denomination, only for them to let you down? That doesn't have to be the end of your faith story. What you need is to rebuild your life on the foundation of Jesus and to be like that careful and wise builder who expects the floods and the winds and the harsh conditions and prepares accordingly. The fool builds for quick comfort today; the wise person wants sturdiness for a lifetime. Ultimately, the wise seek an antifragile life.

In Portland, Oregon, where both of us have spent significant time, there have been warnings that the Pacific Northwest is due for a cataclysmic earthquake. Portland falls within the Cascadia subduction zone, where the Juan de Fuca tectonic plate is sliding beneath the North American plate, making this area vulnerable to a major earthquake; scientists predict an earthquake of 8.0 magnitude or higher will occur imminently. In 2022, the city of Portland developed a program calling on citizens to strengthen their houses to withstand a major earthquake through what's known as seismic retrofitting. While it would have been best and most cost efficient for homes and commercial buildings to have started with seismic resilience in mind, renovating to strengthen the buildings is better than nothing.

Our call to an antifragile faith is an invitation to retrofit your life and faith, reconsidering your foundations and strengthening the whole to secure your standing in a harsh world. A wise builder plans carefully and works slowly and patiently enough to make something that lasts a lifetime. Some who are reading this book may be just starting out in their faith, with the chance to build on the best foundation and construct a solid structure with the strongest materials from the outset. Others (many others, we would imagine) come to this book with some sense of disillusionment and discouragement, burned out and full of doubts and questions about their Christian faith. That's okay; it's why we started a podcast and why we chose to write this book.

In short, it's never too late to aspire to become a wise builder.

TAKE YOUR TIME

Learn to Linger with God

Wise, Powerful, and Slow

Over the following chapters, we will attempt to flesh out what we have come to believe are eight distinct, theologically grounded practices that will help the follower of Jesus cultivate a resilient faith in a turbulent world. In this first chapter, we will commence the journey by arguing that we need to practice a slowed-down, reflective, meditative approach toward faith that resists the pressures to be rushed and to cut corners. In short, we need to take far more time to be formed into the image of Christ.

Amid the revivals of the eighteenth century, the masses began to rekindle a love for and devotion to the Bible across the nation of England. At the time, a famed circuit-riding preacher named John Wesley (1703–91) penned a library of explosive commentaries on Scripture that continue to evoke a love and passion for the Bible in modern hearts and minds. Wesley—a curious student of the biological and physical sciences—was enthralled with the way Genesis depicted the creation of the sun, stars, and moon. His deepening conviction that science and Scripture could learn from each other was giving shape to the tradition that would come after him.[1]

His commentary had a keen eye for biblical details. In one passage, Wesley reflects on the fourth day of creation—the day God formed the luminaries that glistened in the sky above. *Why*, Wesley wonders, *did God create what he did?* While he acknowledged that the purpose of the sun's creation could be plain for the eye to see, what he was left pondering was the elusive meaning behind the existence of the moon. Wesley reflects:

> Some of the uses of the moon we are acquainted with; her causing the ebbing and flowing of the sea; and influencing, with a greater or smaller degree, all the fluids in the terraqueous globe. And many other uses she may have, unknown to us, but known to the wise Creator. But it is certain she had no hurtful, no unwholesome influence on any living creature.[2]

For Wesley, the ever-astute student of the Bible and the physical world, even the less-than-obvious elements of creation are imbued with timeless intentionality, purpose, and meaning. God can't create accidents. There is purpose to all of creation. While the evident usefulness of some parts of creation (in this case, the moon) eluded human reason, hidden in the wise mind of God was a divine purpose for each element he designed. Creation existed only by virtue of God's divine insight, wisdom, and forethought. Similarly, the Genesis account evokes a new awareness of God's singular lordship and power over creation. After having already handcrafted the light, the waters, and the sky, God placed all the stars in the sky. The text of Genesis 1:16 simply reads,

He also made the stars.

As readers of these texts have noted, this reads almost like a throwaway line. It borders on comical: The making of the stars receives the attention of a single line of sacred Scripture. Really? Considering that modern astronomy estimates that some two hundred billion trillion stars exist in the known universe, this limited biblical attention can almost feel irrational to the reader. But Scripture isn't being dismissive. Nor is the Bible being naive. These sacred stories are, in part, testifying to the dynamic, wondrous power of God to create. The paradox is astounding. Humanity couldn't create a single atom from nothing if it tried. But God, the maker of everything, puts all the stars in the sky in the span of one line of biblical literature. Here's how one popular commentator sought to capture Wesley's thought on the matter:

God created the heavens and the earth and didn't even half try.[3]

Clearly, Wesley saw that God's wisdom and power were on full display in making creation. Still, something perplexing also stood out. Though he could have created everything in a single moment, God chose not to. There is no, as it's been called, "point of singularity." Rather, there is a whole week of ongoing creation. Over seven days, God designs the splendor of all that we can see in this glorious creation. God is powerful, but apparently he is *slow* in his execution of that power. And not only slow but even restful. All of creation culminates with a full day of rest. God "finished the work he had been doing . . . [and] rested from all his work" (Gen. 2:2). God stops, observes, and delights in all that he's just made. Why?

Was God overcome with sheer exhaustion? Did making humans take it out of him?

Anything but. The author of Genesis wants to draw the reader's attention to something else. Pay close attention to the word used that describes God's "work" (Hebrew, *mlkh*). Interestingly, *mlkh* served as a word commonly employed to describe ordinary human activity on par with folding laundry, doing dishes, or mowing the lawn. One wouldn't immediately expect such language of ordinary work to be applied to God. As Old Testament commentator Gordon Wenham wisely admits, it is wholly "unexpected that the extraordinary divine activity involved in creating heaven and earth should be so described."[4] But this is a teaching moment: Creation was clearly not difficult for God. He wasn't exhausted. It wasn't demanding for him to form either humans or stars. God creates with an ease akin to someone doing the dishes. God had the unique power to finish everything instantaneously. But, oddly, he did not rush his work. Apparently, true power and true wisdom does not mean acting rashly or hastily.

God, in his wisdom and power, takes his sweet little time.

God doesn't *always* act slowly. There are, to be sure, instances in Scripture where God is described as acting or responding quickly or swiftly. For example, Psalm 147:15 tells us that God's Word "runs swiftly" throughout the world to accomplish his will and desire. The prophet Isaiah goes out of his way to say that God can "swiftly" summon the nations to do his bidding whenever and wherever he wishes (Isa. 5:26). Additional prophetic writings envision God as being "quick to testify" against "sorcerers, adulterers and perjurers, against those who defraud laborers of their wages, who oppress the widows and the fatherless, and deprive the foreigners among you of justice" (Mal. 3:5). In the New Testament, God is quick and eager to forgive the humble sinner who confesses their need (1 John 1:9). God "is not slow," Peter emphasizes, "in keeping his promise" (2 Pet. 3:9). There are undeniable ways in which God acts expediently: when speaking truth and wisdom, summoning the nations, standing against evil, acting on behalf of the oppressed, forgiving sin, and fulfilling what he has promised.

But more often than not, God is described as acting slowly. As we've observed, God (again, in infinite wisdom and power) slowly rolls out creation. Likewise, God is frequently described as being slow to punish by being patient and forbearing final judgment, extending extra time for repentance.[5] God is very often described as being slow to anger.[6] Unlike the gods of the Canaanite religions, the God of Israel was not given to temper tantrums and wrathful flare-ups when someone caught him on the wrong day. This is seen in Exodus 34:6–7:

> The LORD, the LORD, the compassionate and gracious God, slow to anger, abounding in love and faithfulness, maintaining love to thousands, and forgiving wickedness, rebellion and sin. Yet he does not leave the guilty unpunished; he punishes the children and their children for the sin of the parents to the third and fourth generation.

It is worth noting that other parts of Scripture quote this passage more than any other when describing God's character. Two to one, God's slowness is highlighted more than his quickness. God is compassionate, gracious, abounding in love, faithful, and, yes, slow to anger. He isn't in a rush. The wise and powerful God of the Bible is *very, very slow*. We call this the doctrine of the slowness of God. And while one may not find this doctrine discussed in many (if any) theological volumes, it nonetheless pervades the biblical narrative.

Learning to Slow Down

All of this may feel awkward. The slowness of God may come across to the modern person as an odd (or even exotic) way to think about God's nature. But his slowness actually helps illuminate his loving heart. When we observe that he takes his time in making the heavens and the earth—and chooses to rest when finished—it helps us see that God does not suffer divine exhaustion when he creates. God rests for a whole day not because he was *forced* to. God undertakes this work in this way because he is modeling for his creatures what their lives are supposed to look like. God's actions are always invitations. Like a good parent who descends to their knees to be with their child, God is nurturing within humanity (even all of creation) a pattern for life. He is modeling true humanity. The irony is that we believe we can be more effective than God. We try to get everything done as quickly as we can, but the God of the universe slows down and models the importance of enjoying the process. Humans rush, God takes his time.

Any discomfort we have with God's slowness exposes a problem with us, not with God. As theologians and biblical scholars, we are convinced that slowness is a much overlooked attribute of God that the church would do well to embrace in the midst of a dangerously busy and frenetic culture. No doubt, one of the liabilities of actually being embedded in any culture is that God's people can too quickly adopt its ways and assume its pace. Israel's dangerous temptation to "be like all the other nations" (1 Sam. 8:20) around them can tragically become the unspoken mission statement of the church wherever it finds itself. This is especially true in the post-Enlightenment, postindustrial West, where the virtues of speed, productivity, and accomplishment are uncritically accepted as "goods." Too often, God's people in our current moment have adopted an unsustainable pace—leading to endless tales of leadership burnout, rootless discipleship, and impulsive apostasy. God's people can often look more like a multinational corporation that adopts the mottos of efficiency, growth, and expediency with idolatrous fidelity. One author has fittingly called this the "McDonaldization of the church."[7]

In the midst of this, thankfully, many writers have begun to course correct. A flurry of insightful thinkers have sought to reappropriate a healthier pace toward Christian spirituality in recent years. This includes books like *Slow Church* by C. Christopher Smith and John Pattison, which articulates a vision of church life that stands against the effectiveness and expediency of the modern way.[8] Or Kent Annan's *Slow Kingdom Coming*, which seeks to help us adopt a long-term approach toward justice.[9] John Mark Comer's *The Ruthless Elimination of Hurry* and Alan Fadling's *An*

Unhurried Life and *A Year of Slowing Down* have offered a generative approach to slowed-down Christian spirituality.[10]

This slowed-down spirituality emerges as a core theme of the late pastor, theologian, and biblical scholar Eugene Peterson's theological legacy. Peterson did not see slowing down as merely a good idea. Rather, it was a prophetic way of life. Why? For one, Peterson observed, busyness has a way of overburdening Christian leaders—the sad result being that God's own people take a back seat to growing the organization. The tangible love of neighbor, Peterson writes, is often the "first casualty" of one's ordination.[11] Leading a church can often be a job most hostile to actual pastoral work. This was the orienting message of his book *The Contemplative Pastor*, where Peterson contends that the culture of a congregation is most shaped in day-to-day life (what he calls life "in-between Sundays")—in the life and rhythms of its pastor. If a pastor embraces a slowed-down life with God, they can lead the church to do the same. Conversely, the busy pastor becomes a threat to the life of the church. Such a pastor has "no right preaching faith by grace and not by works," Peterson writes, "if their calendar is an altar to workaholism."[12]

Others have even considered slowing down as a method for renewing missions. For example, Reverend H. Scott Holland wrote a short article in the late nineteenth century titled "The Slowness of Mission Work." In it, he discusses what he calls the "terrible slowness of God in creation" and how it should shape the church's practice of sharing the gospel:

The Author of nature is always deliberate in His operations, and attains His natural ends by slow, successive steps, and any one who is surprised at the slowness of God in converting the world, has failed to understand the simplest revelation which God has made of Himself in the world of nature and in the world of man. And then, we remember that this patient slowness of God is the standard measure of man's worth in the sight of God. . . . Man is

23

worth taking all that time in the making, and all that time in the converting. He is worth waiting through all the long centuries for, if only he be won at the end. It is we who are despising ourselves, and despising man, when we think that God will handle him as we might handle a harvest-field, with rough, abrupt methods, mechanical and external, as if, by sudden, violent action, God could sweep in this creature of His, and make him what He chooses.[13]

As God took time in creating, Holland contends, the church should take a long-term approach toward evangelizing the neighbor. The task of evangelizing the world cannot be finished quickly or overnight. It is hard not to agree that our fast-paced way of life inhibits engaging in true relationships. This echoes a point Tony Horsfall makes in his book *Working from a Place of Rest*. Pointing to the story of Jesus with the woman at the well in John 4, Horsfall notes that the entire story could happen only because Jesus stops and takes a break to rest. "Everything that happens in this story happens because Jesus was doing nothing," he writes. "We can learn to work and minister as Jesus did, from a place of rest."[14] It is certainly difficult to love people when you have no time to do so.

Others have considered the importance of slowing down for Christian academics and intellectuals. We are all too familiar with how compulsive busyness can disastrously diminish one's thinking. We make unwise decisions and fail to reflect on what we are doing, living out of impulse rather than intention. In her book *Too Busy?*, scholar Alice Fryling discusses the temptation Christian academics face to produce too much too quickly out of an obsessive desire to contribute, to be seen as wise by colleagues, or to prove or accomplish something. Theologians and biblical scholars alike—in an effort to please the academy—can pimp out their sacred gifts for reputation or accomplishment. Fryling's words cut to the bone:

We want to impress ourselves and others with all we do and all we can produce. We take God-given gifts, push them beyond their

limits and make them sources of pride. . . . Our lips say that we
want to honor God, but the truth may be that we want to show off
our gifts or look impressive to others.[15]

Fryling wisely contends that we need to slow down and do
good intellectual work from a place of peace. Such margin helps
us discern our true motivations. Are we writing and producing
because we seek to glorify God with the gifts he has given us? Or do
we do it because we desire to be known as smart and prodigious?

Authors like those mentioned above reveal not only a deep
need but a renewed interest in slowing down to work alongside
God in whatever we are doing. Their works bring us great joy, and
we are equally convinced that books, resources, and thinkers like
these are producing exceptionally helpful food for thought that
we need to slowly consider. Still, so much more needs to be said
on the topic. Just as we need to learn to slow down our lives, our
calendars, and our patterns of life, we also need to learn to slow
down our thinking to live at a rhythm that makes space for a life
that can truly meditate on God. This will no doubt put us out of
step with the world. But that is no problem, because we are not
meant to look like the world. As Michael Harper pointedly reflects,

> After two millennia of Christian history, the worst judgment that
> the world can pass upon the Church is that she has become a faith-
> ful reflection of the world itself.[16]

From Loitering to Lingering

We admit that embracing slowness is *hard*. But slowness trans-
forms us. One of our favorite theologians, Dr. John Goldingay,
served for decades as a professor of Old Testament theology.
Goldingay reached the pinnacle of his scholarly discipline, but
he also has enjoyed an equally remarkable and fruitful personal
life. Among the many facets of Goldingay's biography that has

left an impact on both of us is his marriage to Ann Goldingay, a woman John loved and shared life with for over forty years until her death in 2009 from health decline due to multiple sclerosis.

Goldingay vulnerably wrote about their journey in retrospect. In a short book titled *Remembering Ann*, John recounts both their shared life through many hard years and the grief he experienced in her passing.[17] The depth of his sadness and lament reflects the gravity of their love. He writes at length about what he learned from Ann about knowing God and how to live well in God's world—even when she was bound to a wheelchair and hardly able to move. He transparently admits how he often lacked the patience needed to care for his wife and how, perhaps, he had paid her too little attention because of her inability to converse.

As she neared her final days, John's awareness of Ann's powerful ministry to visiting students became increasingly clear. Students would observe her stillness, coming to appreciate—and even learn from—how Ann's condition gave her the gift of living her life slowly. Ann had come to meditate on a line from Amy Carmichael, "In acceptance lieth peace." By this point, Ann could hardly move. But her stillness brought peace and contemplation to those who visited her. Writing directly to Ann after her passing, John comments, "You taught people to enjoy life and to stop and look and wait and watch and accept and be."[18]

From that season of life, one story stood out in John's memory. Two friends named Sue and Phil had invited John and Ann on a canal boat ride. Despite this being a near impossibility given Ann's condition, they risked giving it a go. John remembered that he was surprised at just how slow the boat was moving. He expected a brisk ride, but it felt as if it was barely drifting forward. He confesses, "This drove me mad. I could cope with standing still or moving at eighty miles per hour, but not with a canal boat's snail-like slowness." But he could tell Ann was *loving* it. John wanted the thrill of going fast, but Ann liked going slow so she could take in everything around them; she could observe every blade of grass.

"I realized how people who live more slowly," John concluded, "can get more out of life."[19]

Ann did not choose the debilitating disease that slowly stole her mobility and mental acuity. But when she began to accept her situation, she found God in the slowness of life. As she did, others (like John and his students who visited her) began to see and experience God afresh by living their lives at Ann's pace. John and Ann's story, in part, is a testimony to the power of slowness.

Thankfully, slowness is being remembered by the church. And this is a step toward healing. It's no mistake that of the Ten Commandments given in Exodus 20, only one begins with the word "remember." And that is the command to keep the Sabbath day holy. God knew that slowing down would be the one commandment humans would likely forget. Like John on the canal boat ride, we can grow frustrated and bored with slowness. We find ways to do things fast, downloading mapping apps to get places without detours or paying more for overnight mail. At amusement parks, visitors pay to get on rides without waiting in line. In many cases, getting things done faster is desirable. But it seems that a world that automatically presumes the goodness of doing things quickly tends to create people who want *everything* to go faster. Slowness is perceived as a disease, a problem, an issue to be fixed.

Even the English language is skeptical and suspicious of slowness. A simple smattering of synonyms for the word "slow" reveals much about the cultural values of American life. Words like "sluggishness," "apathy," "lethargy," and "languidness" expose many of our assumptions. Consider, for instance, how the English language is devoid of positive language for the act of simply waiting around a place for no good reason. In fact, the one word we do have for it is not only negative but is an illegal activity in some instances: loitering. In some environments, Jesus would have been arrested for loitering around the well to wait for a good conversation.

Yet, ironically, we are willing to pay to get some things slowly or for something to last a long time. We would all love it if chewing gum lasted longer. Or for the back massage to last another hour. If you're having a life-giving conversation with a good friend, you don't want it to go by quickly; you want to savor it, you want time to stand still, to go *slowly*. Imagine sitting on the beach in Hawaii—the smell of the air, the warm breeze, the soothing sounds of the waves. You never want to leave, you long to stay forever, you want to soak it all in. Speed is not the premium. Turns out, slow is not always bad.

Are there any words that capture a good kind of slowness? There are "linger" and "savor." Both mean taking an event or experience slowly, enjoying every last bit of it. There is the deep feeling of not wanting something to end. Try to recall memories of all-night conversations with a best friend or watching your kids play sports. Or a really great music concert—the energy, the sounds, the communal joy. Those times when we are prone to linger are moments that we hold precious, where life is lived to its fullest, where life seems good and right and joyous.

Part of the work of this moment for the church is to relearn the sacred art of lingering, of slowing down and taking more time. To replace the assumptions that we must move faster and get things done more expediently. The church, we believe, should be the place where people learn what Peterson calls "the unforced rhythms of grace,"[20] a place where simply waiting on God and on one another is no longer seen as loitering but as lingering.

The Slow Work of God

We must learn to embrace slowness because it is the way that God most often chooses to work in our lives. God takes his time—not only with the universe but with our own stories. This is perhaps one of the most recognizable qualities new disciples of Jesus begin to notice. When a person places their faith in Jesus, they will immediately begin to see that the journey of deep formation is difficult, challenging, and, at times, painstakingly arduous. One of our undergraduate students who had become a Christian while at university asked early on in their faith journey, "Why this whole life thing? Why doesn't God just take us to heaven when we believe in Jesus? Why do we actually have to live the rest of our lives? What is gained in all this struggle?"

This is a critical question. Why doesn't God simply take us to heaven the minute we believe in Jesus? Why is God so slow? A little theology may prove helpful. Theologians distinguish between two critical experiences in our life with God: conversion and salvation. Conversion is that moment when we make a decision to turn to Christ to find our life, hope, and future. Sure, there may be a process that has led up to any conversion story. But conversion, in Christian theology, is a moment of crisis when we decide to turn to God. The conversion moment or process is one of utmost importance for the follower of Jesus. For example, Paul reminds the Thessalonian Christians how at one important moment they "turned to God from idols to serve the living and true God" (1 Thess. 1:9).

But we must not treat conversion as the *end* of the Christian life. Rather, conversion is the *beginning* of the salvation experience. If conversion is the beginning of the process, salvation is God working out our conversion in our lives. Sadly, in many Christian circles, the two become conflated. It is assumed that when someone turns to faith in Jesus, they are fully saved—in the sense that nothing else is required. But salvation in the New Testament is more than just a conversion experience. Salvation is the lifelong journey of becoming more and more like the image of Christ through the power of the Holy Spirit. Right after Paul mentions the conversion of the Thessalonian Christians, he adds that after that decision they now "wait for his Son from heaven" (1 Thess. 1:10). That is, their lives begin on a path that ends with complete communion with the Savior, Jesus Christ. The Christian life on earth before Christ's return is lived on that path. Sometimes Paul refers to salvation as something that is accomplished in the past (Eph. 2:5), but often he talks about the Christian life itself as *being saved*, life lived on the slow road leading to finality with Christ (1 Cor. 1:18; 2 Cor. 2:15).

Think again of a college education. Every year at graduation ceremonies around the world, graduates walk across a stage and have their names spoken out loud in front of their peers and parents. People clap. And they return to their seats. Students pay with their time, money, and effort to undertake this journey. For most, four (or, for others of us, five or six) years of pain, toil, late-night work, struggle, disappointment, and textbooks have led to this moment. But why? Why don't they just give you a diploma when you pay for it rather than forcing you to go through the education part?

A good education isn't about just one thing. It is about more than acquiring information (although that is part of it) or graduating. If an education were merely about information, then thousands of dollars could be saved by simply watching a bunch of YouTube videos or digital lectures, or reading a lot of books. Nor is the only goal of an education to get the diploma and experience the graduation ceremony. Getting an education is about much more than making a better income in one's career. As important as that is, an education should also form one's character. These are all elements of the whole process. Education is intended to transform the whole person into someone who can handle the complexities and difficulties of human life.

We like to say that conversion takes a second but salvation takes a lifetime. To enter by faith through the work of the Spirit necessitates that the same Spirit continually bestow us with the strength to continue having faith in Christ's work. This ongoing work is what Philip Melanchthon called *conversio continuata*—the "continual conversion" of our whole person to God.[21] What began as an event of grace becomes a constant, ongoing, never-ending movement of grace that leads to one's finished salvation. That conversion and salvation are not the same thing is why Paul would write to a group of converted Christians in Romans 13:11 that "salvation is *nearer* now than when [you] first believed." And why Paul would tell the church in Philippi to "work out your salvation with fear and trembling" (Phil. 2:12). Their conversion stories had begun. But there was so much more God had to do within them. If conversion and salvation were the same, these statements would never have been written in the way they were.

Which returns us to the question: Could God simply take us to heaven when we believed? Could the process be quicker? Sure— just as God could have put the finishing touches on the universe in a millisecond. And God *could* immediately take us to heaven the way he did with Enoch and Elijah before they died. But God rarely works this way. God undeniably has the capacity to do whatever he desires to do. But as we saw in creation, our God of wisdom and power doesn't always work that way. He most often does a slow work in our lives. And that work is preparing us for something extraordinary. It is interesting to note how the New Testament describes the future of the Christian after their earthly existence. We hear snippets of this vision in the words of Paul:

> If we died with him,
>   we will also live with him;
> if we endure,
>   we will also reign with him. (2 Tim. 2:11–12)

Note the word "reign." Paul is clearly echoing something Jesus had himself told the disciples in Luke 22:30, saying, "So that you may eat and drink at my table . . . and sit on thrones, judging the twelve tribes of Israel." We will reign with Christ? And sit on thrones? Historic Christian doctrine has held that in the new creation, Christians will be given the role of ruling and reigning. This is often called the "doctrine of the future reign of the church." This is our future. God's people will take the positions of power that Adam and Eve forsook when they were deceived by the serpent in Genesis 3.

We're just not quite ready for it yet. Sin keeps us from being the kinds of people who can handle such power and authority. An important part of our life in the here and now is preparation in wisdom and maturity for what is to come. The apostle Paul had to call out the immaturity of the Corinthian church for many reasons, not least of which was their habit of taking one another to court with petty lawsuits aimed at the public shame and mockery of their opponents (1 Cor. 6:1–11). Paul was almost speechless and aghast as he confronted the sheer audacity of their behavior: "Do you not know that the Lord's people will judge the world? . . . Do you not know that we will judge angels?" (vv. 2, 3). His point was this: If you can't reasonably judge disputes in trivial matters, how in the world would you be able to judge heavenly matters? Paul's comments reveal two important things: Humans were created in the image of God with incredible power and potential, but even Christians aren't preloaded with perfect wisdom and maturity. We need to grow up into the full maturity of Christ, our model. We are designed to reign with Christ, but Paul took sixteen chapters to remind the Corinthians that this would not happen in an instant.

As Dallas Willard brilliantly writes, the purpose of our formation into the image of Christ is that we are undergoing the slow work of "training for reigning."[22] God is using this long, difficult, arduous life of following Jesus as a way to suit us to our future task—a task we simply are not ready for. The slow work of God is preparing us for our future assignment of ruling and reigning.

Were we to immediately be taken to heaven upon conversion, we wouldn't be prepared to handle our new responsibilities. We have all read the stories of people who suddenly receive a massive inheritance or gain instantaneous fame and eventually burn out, blow it all, or end up murdering someone. The stories are real. A disproportionate number of people who have won the lottery eventually descend into self-destruction. Sudden wealth syndrome is a real phenomenon.[23] And it is a problem. The problem isn't the money, fame, or power that comes with sudden wealth. It is that sinful human beings do not know how to handle such incredible gifts. God is preparing us through a life of slow and difficult struggle. Exercising power and authority well requires proper preparation. This is important for a people who have a track record of destroying whatever Eden they are given.

The Parable of the Good Soil and the Slow Seed

Consider how quickness is presented as a liability in one of the parables of Jesus. In the parable of the sower—one of Jesus's first and most memorable teachings—he says,

> A farmer went out to sow his seed. As he was scattering the seed, some fell along the path, and the birds came and ate it up. Some fell on rocky places, where it did not have much soil. It sprang up quickly, because the soil was shallow. But when the sun came up, the plants were scorched, and they withered because they had no root. Other seed fell among thorns, which grew up and choked the plants. Still other seed fell on good soil, where it produced a crop—a hundred, sixty or thirty times what was sown. Whoever has ears, let them hear. (Matt. 13:3–9)

How should this mysterious saying be interpreted? Certainly, the intrigue of the crowd would not be satiated by this teaching. To the crowds, Jesus never seems to give a satisfying interpretation to his teachings. But privately, in turning to the disciples who have ears to hear, he unpacks some of the most remarkable truths.

Jesus is teaching about receptivity to the kingdom of God. Just as different types of soil affect the growth of seeds, different kinds of hearts respond differently to the same teaching. Jesus explains that some hearts remain entirely unreceptive, likening them to soil from which the evil one quickly removes the seeds before they can take root. Conversely, other hearts are like good soil, where the message can be absorbed, be integrated into a welcoming environment, and develop strong roots that ensure health and resilience. These hearts ultimately bear fruit, yielding vitality and abundance akin to luscious berries or sweet cherries, signifying flourishing and fertility.

However, there exists another type of inhospitable soil. Jesus explains that some seeds fall on seemingly decent ground, but it is surrounded by thorns. These thorns symbolize the suffocating worries of life, such as financial concerns, work responsibilities, and health anxieties. These burdens can weigh us down significantly. While everyone faces these kinds of problems, certain individuals become obsessively preoccupied with making their lives appear neat, orderly, and controlled. They focus on removing the thorns instead of nurturing the plant. Consequently, the seed is deprived of the opportunity to thrive. This seed never stood a chance.

Finally, Jesus talks about the seed that falls on rocky soil. This ground looks natural and healthy, but it isn't soft or rich enough to allow for life to grow and flourish. On the surface it appears okay, but Jesus says it lacks depth; it's too shallow, he explains. The seed does open up, and stalks shoot up quickly, but without thick, deep roots they just can't handle threats, such as the hot, dry sun. Not long after these plants begin life, they rapidly wither and die. Jesus mentions that when we see these plants as people, the sun represents hardships and suffering. These rocky believers are like new Christians who immediately fall in love with Jesus; they experience a whirlwind romance with the gospel and the church, but when things get tough, when the honeymoon is over, they just can't find a reason to stick around. When Jesus explains this to his disciples, he mentions that rocky believers clearly know joy— they feel really good about the good news, at first. They get high on the drug of spirituality and experience the ecstasy of letting go of their baggage from the past, but when it is time to settle into less feel-good rhythms of faith and discipleship, they vanish as quickly as they sprouted.

This is the danger of what we call "spiritual limerence." A helpful way to think about this by comparison is how marriage psychologist John Gottman describes the natural stages of romantic relationships. Most romance begins with what he calls "limerence," the excitement and infatuation of falling in love with another person. But relationships start to become tested when that phase wears off. That is often when counseling and therapy are needed. The second phase, according to Gottman, is "building trust," where both members of the couple have to answer hard questions about being there for each other and about real commitment, even when things don't feel good. Finally, when a couple has found their circle of trust and security, they can develop a strong and resilient foundation of "commitment and loyalty" (phase three). Here's Gottman's critical point: If all we have is limerence, the relationship ain't gonna last very long.[24] It's true for all people. And apparently for spiritual plants too.

One of the warning signs of these rocky believers is that they try to grow up too fast; they want to jump from one joy to another, and their relationship with God and their understanding of the gospel and the kingdom lacks depth: no roots, no maturity. Jesus doesn't come right out and say it, but what makes the good soil so hospitable is that it takes all the steps to make sure the seed has what it needs for growing up big and healthy and strong and fruitful, and that process happens slowly. By the end of the parable, Jesus has wowed the audience and blown the listeners' minds with this miraculous plant that can produce one hundred perfect pieces of fruit. When we contrast that with the rocky soil, it has to be the case that this good soil did it right by doing all the necessary and good things carefully and slowly. There is nothing inherently wrong with being fast or inherently good about being slow. We should be *quick* to listen but *slow* to speak, right? But often, being too quick is harmful because it doesn't take the necessary time to do things right, and being slow is better because it allows for care, planning, and deep attentiveness. So, in a sense, one of Jesus's very first teachings is about the virtue of being slow. Be the good soil. Plan. Cultivate. Enrich. Fertilize. Know where the sun is. Know where the shade is. Add water. Pull weeds. Remove big stones. Take your time. The goal in the end is the best and most healthy fruit, not cheap and quick nourishment.

Tradition has often called this teaching the parable of the sower. Jesus seems to call it that in Matthew 13:18: "Listen then to what the parable of the sower means." Technically, though, in the Greek language that appears in Matthew, it is about a particular action. Thus, a more accurate translation would be, "Listen then to what the parable of the *sowing* means." If you read the parable carefully, Jesus doesn't actually tell us anything about the sower. Is it supposed to be God? An angel? Chance? Even fate? We don't know, because in Jesus's parable that's not where the action is. Jesus's focus, it appears, is on the ground. The parable is about where the seed falls and what happens to the seed. Jesus wants his disciples to have hearts like good soil and the seed to be slow, taking its time to grow in the best conditions so that the plant can eventually be so healthy that it can withstand the harshest conditions and produce the most nutritious and appetizing fruit. That's what "slow theology" is really all about. Slow means nothing unless it means being good soil for Jesus to settle into in our lives. So a better title for this story might be the parable of the good soil and the slow seed.

Christ the Walker

The parable invites us to slowly receive, take in, and meditate on what God has said. While we may receive it with eagerness, we must take much time and energy to build our lives on it. While we are convinced that the church needs to slow down in its rhythms, mission, and life, we also believe that there is one more area that needs to be slowed down: our theology. We contend that one of the ways that a follower of Jesus is properly formed in their life is not by rushing from idea to idea, thinker to thinker, conclusion to conclusion. We would like to suggest that just as we need to slow down our lives and our churches, we are experiencing a desperate need to slow down in how we think about God. We need slow *theology*.

In recent years, we have seen the dangers of a church that does not know how to slow down in the way it thinks about God. This can include, but is not limited to, the following:

Everyday Christians experience increasing demands on their time and have little space or energy to meditatively take God's Word seriously. Without this, our spiritual lives are malnourished and we will not live fully into God's desires for our lives.

Followers of Jesus increasingly feel the pressure to respond to the theological and cultural crises of the day with novelty and insight. These pressures, as real as they are, have created a culture of reactivity rather than responding out of faithfulness and integrity. We hit Send way too quickly.

We are faced with too many decisions every day. The decision paralysis that comes as a result means that we tend to discern with immediacy. Rather than praying about what God would say, we shoot from the hip.

The information age has provided us with questions about God, faith, and the Bible that many have never had to really consider. The demand to "find answers" has driven an entire cottage industry of blogs, podcasts, and writings that purport to give us immediate revelation.

Cultural pressures to bend on core Christian doctrines often use shame, guilt, and emotional coercion to win their battles. Before long, we end up making theological decisions for emotional reasons rather than cultivating a life of faithful patience under the truths of God that transcend time and space.

We all wish we could know about God instantaneously. That the infinite could be attained in a moment. Our technological age tempts us to think we can. A podcast here, a book there, an easy digestible tweet. But just as God takes his time to show us what we should do, we must resist the urge to do instantaneously what God chooses to take his time to do.

In evangelical and Protestant culture, we can tend to have a disproportionately high view of the role of the local pastor—and, by extension, personalities and celebrities. While we should be shaped by holy people, we can often believe what our favorite Christian celebrity says simply because they said it.

These are difficulties. And we could easily go on. But these challenges and realities have placed on us the need to reconsider how we think about God in a fast-paced world. Slow theology is about wanting things to slow down not just when life is really good but all the time, because life itself is a gift, and every moment holds potential for wonder if we become attentive to the richness of the world around us that we tend to miss when we are in a hurry.

As the parable of Jesus instructs, we can receive something too quickly without responsibly taking into account what we are receiving. Is it possible to believe something too quickly? Indeed, it is. We would be wise to learn from that ancient cautionary tale of the first humans in Eden in the way they respond to the words of the serpent who has slithered into the garden. Upon being told by the serpent that they should eat from the prohibited tree of the knowledge of good and evil, they quickly receive (and act on) his deceptive instruction. *Too* quickly. Their decision to believe his words would pave a path that would lead to the rebellion of the entire world. Had they stopped, reflected, and thought carefully about the words that God had given to them, would the rebellion of the humans have ever taken place? Indeed, they believed too quickly the message of the serpent. And too quickly forgot God's nourishing words.

Similarly, Paul chides the churches in and around Galatia for turning from the gospel to what he calls the "works of the law." One can sense Paul's anger—especially when compared to his other letters. In fact, Galatians remains his only letter in which he does not say a word of gratitude to God for the church at the beginning of the letter. Paul is angry. And his anger is connected to one thing: "I am astonished that you are so *quickly* deserting the one who called you to live in the grace of Christ and are turning to a different gospel— which is really no gospel at all. Evidently some people are throwing you into confusion and are trying to pervert the gospel of Christ" (1:6–7). The word "quickly" is important here. Someone or some group has slithered its way into the churches and is sowing a word of disruption, robbing them of their joy in Christ. The problem for the Galatians? They believed too quickly. Later in the letter, Paul accuses them of being "bewitched" (3:1). He doesn't mean this literally, as if the other teachers had put them in a trance with a hex. Paul is commenting on how their *quickness* to believe these lies is so inexplicable that they must have been hypnotized! Put simply, like fools they rushed in, and their brains didn't have enough time to catch up.

Yet, at the same time the New Testament gives instances in which Christians do not believe fast enough. Following the resurrection, two disciples are making the long walk from Jerusalem to Emmaus. Little did they know, Jesus would come and speak to them incognito along the way. Appearing to play dumb, Jesus asks these disciples what was going on. Unaware, they comically explain to Jesus what had happened to Jesus. Then, Jesus explains to them that what has happened had to take place. It had been written. Luke simply writes,

> He said to them, "How foolish you are, and how slow to believe all that the prophets have spoken! Did not the Messiah have to suffer

these things and then enter his glory?" And beginning with Moses and all the Prophets, he explained to them what was said in all the Scriptures concerning himself. (Luke 24:25–27)

What matters most is not necessarily the speed with which we believe in something—one can err on either side. What is most important is the truthfulness of what one is believing. This is why taking one's time can be so important. We often need time to discern whether the message we are receiving is of God or not. The two Emmaus-bound disciples were not being slow in a good way, carefully weighing the truth with penetrating discernment. Their slowness was a sign of not being able to make sense of how Scripture had been pointing to the suffering and self-giving Messiah all along. We must be slow in a careful investigation of the truth but quick to believe once we know the truth!

Years ago, Japanese theologian Kosuke Koyama wrote an interesting little book called *Three Mile an Hour God*, in which he looked at the speed at which the average person walks.[25] The average person walks three miles an hour. This is important given that nearly 90 percent of the stories that take place in the New Testament occur as Jesus and his disciples are walking somewhere. Koyama wrote an entire book about the fact that Jesus—a true human like us—was very slow. Jesus did not undertake his mission quickly. The incarnation is God walking around for thirty-three years at a very slow and rhythmed pace. God, in the incarnation of Jesus, saves the world by embracing the slow life.

Which brings us back to creation. Imagine for a moment that you had the chance to go and sit in a chair and watch God roll out the universe. Knowing that God is all-powerful and can do whatever he wants and in the way he wants, your first impression might have been that the God of the universe is remarkably slower than one would expect. Likewise, imagine for a moment that you had the opportunity to spend three years watching an upstart Messiah who you knew was divine make his way to Jerusalem to die on the cross and rescue the world. Your impression, we believe, would have been the same. Jesus took his time to establish something new, just as the Father took time with his creation.

It's never wise to try to be faster than God.

EMBRACE THE THEOLOGICAL JOURNEY

Take the Long View of Faith

The What of Theology

As we've discussed, taking our time is a critical component of cultivating a resilient faith. Our love for Christ must be developed slowly and carefully. In this chapter, we will explore another key principle: learning to embrace the journey of the Christian faith. To begin, it's going to be helpful to back up and address more fundamental questions related to faith: What is theology? And what is its goal? Let's start with the first question. The word "theology"—lexically rooted in the Greek words *theos* ("God") and *logos* ("word")—is the study and contemplation of the nature of God, divinity, and the transcendent. This broad definition serves a purpose, as it encompasses the human work of contemplating the nature of God.

In its broadest sense, theology includes any such reflection. When a Buddhist contemplates detachment, spirituality, or nonviolent pacifism, they are engaging in theology. A Muslim practices theology when reflecting on the messages they believe were received by Muhammad. An agnostic does theology when claiming that if God exists, he is unknowable. Even the atheist engages in theology when asserting the nonexistence of a divine being. Theology is the human enterprise of considering and contemplating the nature of the divine, irrespective of one's specific beliefs or traditions. In this way, everyone is a theologian.[1]

Everyone does theology on some level. There's not a single person in human history with the mental capacity to do so who has not thought about God's existence, what happens after death, why material exists, and who must be behind everything that's been made. Everyone is a theologian because everyone thinks something about God. But not every theologian undertakes the task of theology with Christian convictions.

Now, there's obviously a noticeable chasm between theology in general and Christian theology. Theology in the Christian sense undertakes the task with distinct convictions and often quite countercultural aims. For the person seeking to follow the way of Jesus, theology means giving our total reflection, thought, and consideration to the divine persons of the Father, Son, and Holy Spirit as revealed through the biblical storyline. This considerably sharpens the focus of theology—in more ways than one. Most importantly, it draws our attention to an actual person. Consider Alister McGrath's apt definition of Christian thought: "Theology is the reflection upon God whom Christians adore and worship."[2]

The focus in Christian theology is not on just *any* god. The aim of Christian theology is the adoration of the God who was revealed as a real human with a real name—Jesus Christ.[3] Christian theology must always be harnessed to the history of this particular person and must seek to follow him in all things. Just as Jesus called his disciples to "follow me" (Matt. 16:24) in their habits, practices, and daily lives, he also calls us to do the same with our thinking. This is Christian theology: human thinking that has abandoned everything to pursue the truth under the tutelage of God the Creator, Jesus the Christ, and the Spirit of holiness.

The Bible, therefore, plays an inescapable role in historic, faithful Christian theology. Far too often our thinking can get *ahead* of Jesus. The lurking danger that this presents is illuminated in Paul's warning to the Corinthian church against running ahead and allowing their feeble judgments to take precedence over God's final judgment. God always has the final say.[4] Jesus even scolds Peter: "Get behind me, . . . [for] you do not have in mind the concerns of God" (Matt. 16:23). And John provides the clearest of warnings to the churches around Ephesus in his second epistle: "Anyone who runs ahead and does not continue in the teaching of Christ does not have God; whoever continues in the teaching has both the Father and the Son" (2 John 1:9). The dangerous tendency of all human thinking, judgment, and theology is that it can often run ahead of Christ. A true and faithful Christian theology follows the real Jesus. Scripture is what holds the feet of theology to the fire of the Spirit. "Do not," Paul writes, "go beyond what is written" (1 Cor. 4:6).[5]

The longer we observe Christ with our heads and hearts in the Bible, the more our bad, half-baked, and errant theology comes to light. Scripture gives us the constant gift of theological humility—to the degree that we are willing to boldly acknowledge that our own thinking about Christ isn't always right. Put simply, our theology isn't always the same as the truth. We are often wrong. Those with a high view of and deep love for the Bible (like ourselves) can often fail to appreciate this. We spend much of our lives presuming that something must be true because we happened to have believed it for a long time or received it from someone we looked up to. Any preacher worth their salt has learned this lesson time and again whenever they read their old sermons. In revisiting homilies from years past, we are sometimes left wondering how we could have ever spoken such half-baked truths knowing what we know now—and even shocked that someone dared to give us the microphone.

Each of our own histories is chock-full of personal foibles. So why should we be so arrogant as to assume we have overcome this tendency? If we have been wrong in the past, it would seem logical to accept that we will also be wrong now and in the future. Christian history is loaded with tale after tale of failed starts, errant interpretations, and off-kilter theologies that have not served the gospel of Jesus Christ. Acknowledging the truth that one's theology does not always correspond to who God actually is remains a critical angle to understanding *how* a Christian should do theology. Theologian Roger Olson wisely writes, "Theology means reflection on divine revelation in order to believe rightly and understand what is rightly believed."[6]

Let's focus on one core component of Olson's definition of theology. Theology itself is not divine revelation. Rather, theology is "reflection on divine revelation." God and what God says is the revelation. From a historic Christian perspective, theology is one's study, reflection, and thought on the triune God in the Father, Son, and Holy Spirit. But that study, reflection, and thought is often found to be wanting. Theology is one's reflection on God's nature. But this does not always correspond to God. What a finite human may think about God will always fall short of the majestic glory that is God's alone. As we all have experienced, we sometimes discover that our thinking falls gravely short of God's true self. "All have sinned and fall short of the glory of God," Paul writes in Romans 3:23. Is it unfair to wonder if the same could be said about our thoughts toward him?

Loving God entails recognizing that our thoughts about him need some work. This posture of the heart is the beginning of the best theology—and truest of wisdom. Reformed theologian Richard

Hughes once wrote, "If I confess the sovereignty of God and the finitude of humankind, I confess as well that my reason is inevitably impaired and that my knowledge is always incomplete."[7] If we truly believe in a God who is infinite, perfect, and glorious, then we as finite creatures must humbly concede that our thinking is not.

Which leads us to our second question: What is the *goal* of Christian theology? The goal of theology is never merely theological knowledge. The goal of theology is always an encounter with the living God. A Christian's allegiance is always first and foremost to the person of Jesus Christ—not to their current understanding of him. As such, the work of theology is never the end goal of theology. This kind of theology merely "puffs up" rather than brings us into an experience of Jesus Christ (1 Cor. 8:1).

Theology isn't the goal. But it is the path we must take. In his book *The Parables of Grace*, theologian Robert Farrar Capon seeks to illustrate this distinction by casting theology as a kind of porch in front of someone's house. Nobody lives on a porch, Capon suggests. But in order to come inside a house, the visitor likely has to go *through* a porch. Theology is a porch, the pathway we must take to achieve our goal of encountering God. Thus, we must recognize both the necessity and the frivolity of all theology. As with an airport, we go through it—but we don't stay there.[8]

The goal, then, of theology is not to arrive at self-certitude, arrogance, or hubris. The goal of seeking the truth is to begin to love God, who is himself the truth. "I am the way and the truth and the life," Jesus tells his disciples (John 14:6). To seek the truth is to seek Jesus. There is an intimate relationship between theological rigor and passions of prayer. Theologian Christopher West speaks of the difference between an optometrist and a lover as a helpful way of contrasting the work of studying God and the work of loving him:

> Consider the difference for a woman when her optometrist looks into her eyes and when her husband or boyfriend does so. The

scientist is looking at her cornea and records the scientific facts. The lover is looking at her soul and proclaims something more poetic and inspired (we hope). Does the scientist "disprove" the lover? No. These are simply two perspectives on the same reality.[9]

There is a critical place for study. To love God is to incorporate the facts, the history, and the truths of God. But if we end there, we simply study him. We need to study God, but it should never end there. We must seek, through that study, to also gaze into the eyes of God and find ourselves his beloved. Theology and prayer, then, are not enemies. They should go hand in hand. To truly love a person is to know *about* them. But truly knowing a person also entails loving them as they are.

The Theological Journey

Theology is a journey. To fully appreciate this journey, we must understand that God is both the revealer and the enabler of any knowledge one may possess about him. This is vividly illustrated in Matthew 16:1–16. In a conversation with his disciples, Jesus asks, "Who do people say the Son of Man is?" (v. 13). His disciples, being uncertain, offer a variety of speculations: "Some say John the Baptist; others say Elijah; and still others, Jeremiah or one of the prophets" (v. 14). Clearly, unfounded claims and wild rumors circulated around the growing ministry of Jesus.

The conversation then turns to another disciple who has yet to respond. Jesus directs the same pointed question to Peter. Remarkably, Peter responds accurately and immediately, declaring, "You are the Messiah, the Son of the living God" (16:16). Jesus affirms Peter's insight and emphasizes that this revelation did not come from any human source—Peter's parents, a website, the crowds. No. This revelation had come directly from God.

What remains particularly fascinating about this short exchange is that Peter seems to be unaware of the full extent to which his understanding was spot on until Jesus confirms it. This makes things awkward. It is apparently possible for someone to possess a revelation about God and not be entirely aware that they possess it.[10] This underscores a profound, penetrating truth: Revelation is not merely about God. Revelation is mediated *by* God. God is both the goal and the gatekeeper of theological truth. He is both the source and the means of all revelation. Thus, Christ is not only the subject of Christian theology but also its very method and pathway.

Do not be fooled, however. Peter's moment of clarity did not in the least imply some kind of apostolic infallibility in his understanding. In the very next story after recognizing Jesus as the Messiah, Peter sternly rebukes his master for predicting that he is going to die (Matt. 16:21–23). Furthermore, Peter would later deny Jesus three times on the eve of Christ's death (26:69–75). These failings are just the ones mentioned in Matthew's telling. Knowing who Christ is does not, in any way, mean one has arrived at total truth. Like Peter, we all have partial understanding and must continue to learn and grow in the way of Jesus. None of us have fully arrived.

This lifelong work of learning God is called the "theological journey."[11] This journey entails a constant process of evaluation, reevaluation, and sanctification. It can be seen in some of the church's most consequential theologians, such as Anselm of Canterbury (1033–1109). Anselm was a monk, abbot, philosopher, and theologian who held the important seat of archbishop of Canterbury from 1093 to 1109. One of Anselm's most important works was originally titled *Monologion*. It is an exhaustive argument for the existence of God. The title reveals its content—it is a "monologue" about God's nature, and it has been widely viewed as one of the most important theological works ever written in the church.

Tradition goes, however, that after finishing *Monologion*, Anselm became aware of a distinct problem with his writing process. Anselm had written about God as though God were not present to him as he wrote. Rather than writing *with* God, he wrote *about*

God. Anselm decided to rewrite it—eventually calling it *Proslogion*, meaning "discourse" or "dialogue." The shift in substance, tone, and outlook in the second volume was significant. In fact, one of the most repeated principles in the realm of theology comes from Anselm's *Proslogion*:

> I do not attempt, O Lord, to penetrate Thy profundity, for I desire to understand in some degree Thy truth, which my heart believes and loves. For I do not seek to understand, in order that I may believe; but I believe that I may understand. For I believe this too, that unless I believed, I should not understand.[12]

Anselm had clearly been humbled. And the consequence of this in the realm of theology cannot be overstated. Theology, unlike any other discipline, is one that *begins* with belief, hope, and faith in God. The modern world may say, "I'll believe it when I see it"—assuming that belief follows understanding and empirical evidence. Theology, on the other hand, begins not with experience or with evidence. Theology begins with faith. Theology is not just about the study of God. Theology, as its proper end, is about knowing God himself.

The story of Anselm is likely similar to many of our own. Along the path of following Jesus, we come to discover that some of our thinking has not done justice to the story of Jesus as told in the Bible, or we've believed wrongly, or we've believed in right ideas but in the wrong way. Anselm's journey of rethinking his theology is the journey every follower of Jesus must pick up. If we are called to lay down everything and follow Jesus, that also applies to our theology. We need to turn from sin to follow the righteous ways of Christ. We need to turn from a self-centered existence to a God-centered existence. We need to leave old habits that make us stumble so that we can be free in Christ. Likewise, our thinking, reflection, and theological considerations must constantly go through the journey of being refined and sanctified.

The refinement process in the theological journey for all of us is at the heart of much of the Christian theological tradition. For example, in his *On the Trinity*, Augustine reflects on the call and purpose of theology—and on its weight:

> Let me ask of my reader, wherever, alike with myself, he is certain, there to go with me; wherever, alike with me, he hesitates, there to join with me inquiring; wherever he recognizes himself to be in error, there to return to me; wherever he recognizes me to be so, there to call me back; so that we may enter together upon the path of charity, and advance towards Him of whom it is said, "Seek His face evermore." And I would make this pious and safe agreement, in the presence of our Lord God, with all who read my writings . . . because in no other subject is error more dangerous, or inquiry more laborious, or the discovery of truth more profitable.[13]

For Augustine, nothing is more dangerous or more profitable than endeavoring to think rightly about God. Indeed, thinking about God can be of great importance. But it can also be entirely destructive. Scripture is chock-full of key texts showing us that God is always greater than our thinking about him. The book of Deuteronomy declares,

> The secret things belong to the LORD our God, but the things revealed belong to us and to our children forever, that we may follow all the words of this law. (29:29)

Elsewhere, Scripture reminds us that our thoughts about God do not always reflect who God actually is. As God would say through the prophet Isaiah,

> "For my thoughts are not your thoughts, neither are your ways my ways," declares the LORD. "As the heavens are higher than the earth, so are my ways higher than your ways and my thoughts than your thoughts." (55:8–9)

Or, finally, the wisdom writings of Ecclesiastes say,

> He has made everything beautiful in its time. He has also set eternity in the human heart; yet no one can fathom what God has done from beginning to end. (3:11)

God does reveal himself. But texts like this make it equally clear that he is not *exhaustive* in his revelation to us. God couldn't fully reveal everything. We couldn't handle it.

Just as in his act of creation, God refuses to reveal everything to us in a moment's notice. God takes his time inviting us into the truth of his reality. It is fascinating to note that during the life and ministry of Jesus, the incarnate Son of God did not disclose everything to his disciples. Much was left unsaid. In fact, Jesus seemed to signal that there were certain things he could not disclose because he himself (as a human) did not know them. "But about that day or hour no one knows," Jesus said, "not even the angels in heaven, nor the Son, but only the Father" (Mark 13:32). Apparently, there were some things (such as the return of Jesus) that were not revealed to Jesus by the Father during his earthly life. But why was this information not known by Jesus or disclosed to him? Some knowledge is too high for us to attain. Just as Jesus did not disclose everything to his disciples in his thirty-three years as a human, God does not disclose answers to all our questions today.

This not knowing may feel uncomfortable—especially in a culture shaped by an addiction to acquiring endless information and knowledge. By virtue of the proliferating technology that we have at our fingertips, we are trained from our earliest age that we can find out anything we want to know. We can get our information in written, audio, or visual form whenever we so desire. There are great benefits to such access. But it cultivates within us a distaste for anything that we feel is off-limits or something that we are unable to know for ourselves. People who live in the information age can feel entitled to knowing all things.

God can withhold knowledge of himself for whatever reason he has determined. Yet many people want to know everything and know it right now. But this betrays the way that God reveals himself. He does not bend to our desires or expectations. God will reveal himself when and how he so desires—and not before then.

This may feel as if God is withholding from us unfairly. But it is actually a mark of God's love. Any parent knows this principle intimately. There comes a critical moment in a child's development when it becomes appropriate to begin the conversation about sex. The birds and the bees *need* to be discussed—better in the home and the church than in the classroom. For many parents, in the sex-infused culture in which we find ourselves, it has become necessary to have this conversation earlier than in generations past. If we do not form young minds with a healthy biblical sexuality, they will be formed into the grotesque image of sexuality that our culture offers. Sex must be discussed. Still, it's awkward. It requires wisdom to know when and how that conversation should be had.

In this journey, a wise parent will exercise discernment in determining what should be communicated, the appropriate timing, and the suitable medium for conveying it. Parents who have an appreciation for human development will understand that premature disclosure may lead to a breakdown in the parent-child relationship. Conversely, delaying necessary conversations can result in a child being shaped by harmful influences—especially in the realm of sexuality. Therefore, discussing the birds and the bees necessitates three key elements: the commitment to unveil the truth, the wisdom to choose the right moment, and the child's maturity to handle such truths responsibly. Sharing everything at one moment may actually be harmful to a child's development.

The journey of learning what God is like is similar to the journey of learning about our best friend. Knowing God is not the abstract work of memorizing a bunch of factoids about a person. Knowing God is so much more dynamic than that. In fact, we often settle for knowing things about God without knowing God himself. We have a word for that: "stalker." Many Christian stalkers treat God as a set of propositions and statements rather than a living God. Knowing God is a lifelong journey of learning in the context of a real relationship between two real beings. There will be mistakes, misunderstandings, and wrongheadedness. This, in fact, is the sign that we are on the right journey. If there is a real God—and we are really sinners—then the sign we are actually loving someone outside of ourselves is that we are, from time to time, wrong. Otherwise, it is like we are just loving ourselves.

Theology is, above all, a journey.

John W. de Gruchy (b. 1939) is a theologian most known for his resistance to apartheid in South Africa. His studious and thoughtful reflections on Dietrich Bonhoeffer have spurred on many important conversations about the role and limits of reconciliation in seeking to right wrongs. In a letter written to young theologians, he puts to words the very essence of this journey:

> Yes, indeed, theology is being on a journey into the mystery of life and therefore trying to understand that journey better. . . . [Theology] is entering through the narrow gate that leads us to know the One "in whom we live, move and have our being." Yes, theology is all about getting to know God! And Christian theology, and that is what we are all engaged in, is knowing the God who we believe is revealed in Jesus Christ. Once you say that, then you immediately begin to discover why theology is a journey of "faith seeking understanding," as Anselm has taught us.[14]

Christ has been revealed to us. But the journey of arriving at clarity regarding that revelation is a journey that takes a lifetime. In his book *Answering God*, Eugene Peterson says that Anselm's move from talking *to* God to talking *with* God is one of the most important outcomes of Christian theology—the move from study to a life of prayer.[15]

But like all real journeys, the real experience is often more challenging than we expected. God wants us to pursue him, but it's not as simple as turning on a spiritual GPS. This challenging, arduous journey shapes us. As we mentioned, Japanese author Kosuke Koyama writes about how God came and walked in Christ. This, he believes, should shape the way God forms us:

> I find that God goes "slowly" with his educational process of man. "Forty years in the wilderness" points to his basic educational philosophy. Forty years of national migration through the wilderness, three generations of united monarchy, nineteen Kings of Israel (up to 722 BC) and twenty kings of Judah (up to 587 BC), the hosts of prophets and priests, the experience of exile and restoration. Isn't this rather a slow and costly way for God to let his people know the covenant relationship between God and man? . . . God walks slowly because of his love for us. If he did not love, he would have gone much faster. Love has its speed. It is an inner speed; a spiritual speed.[16]

Deus Absconditus

Have you ever noticed how sometimes in Scripture God wears a disguise or withholds his whole identity when he visits humans on earth? You have that odd story in the Old Testament where the patriarch Jacob was traveling with his family, and when he happened to be alone, a mysterious man started wrestling with him, and they fought all night (Gen. 32:22–25).

Can you imagine that?

Some stranger clotheslines you for seemingly no reason, and you're just rolling around in the dirt in the dark for hours? Finally, the stranger pops your hip out of joint, but you keep at it until he begs you to stop. On top of that, Jacob pleads with the stranger for a blessing, because he realizes this is a divine encounter, maybe also a test. Israel memorialized this event, calling that place Peniel, which means "face of God," because Jacob had the rare privilege of meeting God face-to-face. But *what in the world?* Was this really how Jacob was meant to encounter God? Hours of twilight mud wrestling? This is far from the storybook tales of divine intervention where an angel appears to pull people out of a pit or to fight off a demon and save the day at the last minute.

And then you have the legendary burning bush. It's not as frenetic as Jacob's divine encounter, but still, so many questions. *Why a bush? And why was it burning? How long had it been there? And did it disappear when Moses left?* God could choose any form to take: T. rex, Bigfoot, unicorn, merman—the possibilities are literally endless. But when Yahweh is about to change the fate of Israel forever through Moses and Aaron, he chooses . . . a bush. Yeah, it's burning, that's kinda awesome, but it's still shrubbery. It seems a little bit like God chose a disguise (or, theologians would say, an "indirect theophany") to make people struggle to recognize him. A great example of this is the story of the two disciples on the road to Emmaus. This story takes place after Jesus died and rose from the dead. According to Luke 24:1–12, certain women (such as Mary Magdalene) were present at the tomb and received the news of the resurrection from two angels. They went and told the men, but the men did not believe them. Then the men went to the cemetery to see for themselves, witnessed the empty tomb, but left confused and unsure.

In the very next scene, two unnamed disciples are walking to Emmaus, trying to process what happened to Jesus, disappointed that their movement ended this way. Jesus himself catches up to them and starts to walk with them, but he is in disguise. "What are you discussing together as you walk along?" Jesus asks (Luke 24:17). (We have no idea what kind of disguise he wore, but it's hard not to imagine Jesus in a fake mustache, sunglasses, trench coat, and a wig.) Jesus asks them what is going on—he was clearly playing dumb. The two disciples rehearse the events, concluding that the women claimed that angels told them Jesus was alive, but when the men showed up, there was nothing there and nobody around. Right then, disguised Jesus calls them fools and teaches them how Scripture pointed ahead to these events now transpiring. But, remarkably, Jesus stays in disguise even while explaining Scripture to them. (It's like getting an acting lesson from Meryl Streep, not knowing it was Meryl Streep.) Even when they get to Emmaus, Jesus pretends to be moving on down the road to the next town. The two disciples offer him a place to stay, and he gladly accepts. (Apparently Jesus was really committed to this bit.) Finally, over a meal, Jesus gives thanks, breaks bread, and passes it out, clearly evoking the Last Supper (Luke 22:19). Finally they recognize it is Jesus, and then POOF! Jesus disappears.

Then there's John's story about Mary Magdalene weeping at the tomb, not knowing where they moved Jesus's body (John 20:13–16). John doesn't come right out and tell us Jesus was in disguise, but Jesus doesn't blurt out, "Hey, it's me, your Teacher, Jesus!" He asks, "Woman, why are you crying? Who is it you are looking for?" (v. 15). To be clear, Jesus *knows* the answers to these questions, and Mary responds while still "thinking he was the gardener." Finally, Jesus says to her "Mary," and she instantly recognizes his voice. It's a touching recognition scene, where Mary immediately turns from confused grief to unreserved jubilation, but it still raises the question: *Why did Jesus play along? Why doesn't he reveal himself immediately?*

Why does God sometimes withhold his identity? It's not a new question. Jews and Christians have been pondering this for four thousand years. The good news is that there are some clear answers from Scripture. It has to do with perceiving who God really is, distinguishing the genuine from the false, the authentic from the counterfeit, the one true God from false idols.

The pagan nations made idols, statues of stone or metal or wood, but the one God cannot be captured in an image. History has shown us that people throughout time have been tempted to make gods in their own human image. Sinful people want to worship gods who are just like them but a bit more powerful. But according to the Old Testament, Yahweh did not allow Israel to make these kinds of idols. Part of the reason is that once you get into the idol-making business, you start to dictate not only what the statue looks like but what it is holding (like a sword) and what it is doing (like going to war).

Pretty soon it feels like the craftsperson is making the divine *do* things, and next thing you know the creature becomes the creator. And once you've made a whole statue—thinking through every curve of their robe, texture of their skin, curl of hair, the crack in the wood of their staff—you might just believe you know everything about them. Yahweh did not want to be a "thing" to be seen and known; like a real person, there is no end to the mystery of existence, so the one God wisely forbade Israel from making statues of him. Yahweh reveals himself bit by bit, in relationship, and does not allow Israel access to that intimate knowledge until they are ready. Personal knowledge is a privilege, not a right.

An utterance from the prophet Isaiah has left a major impact on theologians throughout the ages: "Truly you are a God who has been hiding himself" (Isa. 45:15). Isaiah proclaims this in the context of Israel learning not to trust idol-worshiping nations. The Lord was saying to his people that a foreign nation might come and pretend to want to worship Yahweh, but it is a trick. They want to use religion as a tool to get what they want from Israel, but this will be to their shame. In a sense, God hides (or disguises himself) because he doesn't want to be used as decoration or a pawn in their political games. But there may also be a sense in which God hides because he would be too easily ignored if he just stood out there in the open, like an old statue hoping for some visitors and for someone to clean up the cobwebs and shoo away nesting birds. Isaiah 45:15 inspired a theological concept called *Deus absconditus*, also known as the "hidden God." God doesn't hide because he is shy or annoyed by pesky humans. In many ways, God "hides in plain sight" because only the right kind of eyes and ears and hearts will truly recognize him.

Put another way, God hides because he wants to be pursued and found. This is precisely what Yahweh tells Israel when they must accept the harsh punishment of exile. That experience might make it seem like the covenant is no more, like Yahweh is dead to them, and they to him, but Jeremiah proclaims a word of hope from the Lord. Yahweh has a future plan for Israel, to restore them and to have intimate fellowship once again. But they will need to have learned their lesson about waywardness and stiff-necked disobedience. Ultimately, though, Yahweh doesn't want to reject them; he wants to be their God, and they his people: "You will seek me and find me when you seek me with all your heart" (Jer. 29:13) and then "I will be found by you" (v. 14).

Jacob. Moses. The Emmaus-bound travelers. Weeping Mary. It's not that God doesn't want to be known. He visits people precisely *so* he can be known. But the key is this: God wants to be pursued so there can be a deeper knowing. He rewards signs of curious and penetrating faith with a deeper knowledge of who he is. *Will you wrestle all night? Will you take your sandals off and come closer to the fiery bush? Do you feel your heart burning in the company of this stranger? Do you recognize the Rabbi's voice?* God doesn't just want to be *believed in*, like Santa Claus or the tooth fairy. The living God wants to be *known*. Like a baby who, though she doesn't know two plus two, knows *intimately* the face of her mother. Like a sheep who will follow the shepherd's voice without having to look over and double-check. Learning theology is good, it is a gift, and it is necessary for Christian faith and discipleship. But a fruitful life with God cannot be boiled down to acing a theology quiz. It's an active and never-ending pursuit of knowing the God who hides but who wants to be found by us.

The Ecstatic and the Proleptic

Back to the purpose of theology. Why do we do it? This is an integral question. Is theology the journey of arriving at some conclusions about God? Put another way, is theology the journey of finally arriving at a place where we no longer have questions?

58

If it is, then nobody in the biblical storyline appears to have possessed a complete theology. Even following the resurrection of Jesus, there are numerous moments in which the disciples (even after three years with Jesus) continue to have wrongheaded ideas about God. That is to say, arriving at perfect knowledge is not the goal of theology. We can't attain that. The goal of theology is, first and foremost, entering into a satisfying and sanctifying intellectual relationship with God. We are saved by faith. But beliefs—the work of theology—take endless work and effort.

There are distinct levels of this kind of work. First, we say that theology is *proleptic*. By that, theologians mean that the task of all theology is endless seeking and striving—never arriving. The only moment we arrive is when we are face-to-face with Christ. The journey of a theologian (professional or not) entails constant seeking of that which is true, good, and godly. Of course, this does not mean that we never arrive at theological conclusions. We do, and should. In fact, this is one of the goals of theology—to arrive at a satisfying way to think about God's true nature. The purpose of theology is not, in the words of Calvin, "senseless curiosity."[17] We don't seek for seeking's sake. We seek to actually find.

Second, theology is *ecstatic*. By this we mean it is always seeking something outside of oneself, meaning the point is not theology for theology's sake. The point of theology is *God*. Theology assumes that truth is outside of ourselves and needs to be sought outside of ourselves. We are not the truth ourselves.[18] Jesus is the truth. And the Christian life is an endless pursuit to seek the one who created all things.

The Bible does not invite us to merely understand and receive a set of truths or facts. The biblical description of truth is knowledge of the person of truth. The Hebrew word for "truth" is *emeth*, which is to be understood in the context of a right relationship, not merely the possessing of right facts. In fact, Jesus called himself "the way and *the truth* and the life" (John 14:6).

The God Who Chases After Us

Faithful theology and discipleship is a chasing after God, specifically a God who hides but who really does want to be found. At times, God can seem elusive, not because he wants to be left alone but because we must continually learn to put down our idols and run hard after Jesus. Doing theology in the Christian way is not about knowing lots of things about God, it's not about being able to explain the Trinity (good luck with that!), it's not about getting a PhD in biblical studies. Learning is good and a tool of godliness, but theology is foremost about *devotion*, running after God because we are desperate for grace. God's approach to us is like a parent beckoning a toddler to toddle to them. Of course, the loving mother could go over and pick up the child. But it is good and right for the child to struggle to learn how to walk, to go through the challenges, pains, and inevitable mistakes of learning how to move of their own volition toward the beloved. Theology is the amazing chase.

A mystery is hidden within Scripture and theology in that while we toddle to God because we want to know and be known (which is very good), as we pursue God with more wisdom and understanding, it becomes clear that God has really been following and chasing after *us*. We are all too often unaware of the empowering and grace-filled presence of God in our lives. Paul explains that God made the whole world to reflect his glory, and he created people to be in his image "so that they would seek him and perhaps reach out for him and find him, though he is not far from any one of us" (Acts 17:27).

If you've spent any time in American evangelical culture, you know the famous "Footprints in the Sand" story. A believer looks back on their life as footprints in the sand. There is a stretch of beach where there is only one set of prints. The believer asks God with confusion and disappointment, "Why is there only one set of footprints here? Did you leave me?" God answers, "My child, I never left you. Those places with only one set of prints are where I carried you." *Touching.* The inspirational posters and desktop calendars featuring this story are legendary. (Look for them at Big Lots or Dollar Tree.) There are various spoofs on the footprints story. Like when God says, "That was when I carried you . . . and that long groove over there is when I dragged you for a while; one time, I hid you in that little sand hole while I got a hot dog." Another one goes, "That is when I carried you. You can't leave footprints in the sands of time if you're sitting on your butt. And who wants to leave butt prints in the sands of time?"

As cheesy as the footprints posters are, the original concept does resonate with how God is portrayed in the Bible. Another Christian poster from days of old (popularized in the 1980s) does an even better job of portraying the God who chases *us*: Jesus stands at a door, knocking, sometimes accompanied by an inscription of Revelation 3:20: "Behold, I stand at the door, and knock: if any man hear my voice, and open the door, I will come in to him, and will sup with him, and he with me" (KJV). From this perspective, pursuing God is less about running around in a frantic game of hide-and-seek and more like scanning the room where you *already are*, carefully looking for clues of God's invisible but transformative presence. God is present, willing, and eager to know us more deeply, but he wants to be invited into closer intimacy and communion.

THINK SLOWLY

Applying Sabbath to Our Theology

The Quick and the Slow

Please don't misunderstand the intent behind this book. One might mistakenly conclude that the follower of Jesus is discouraged from making quick theological decisions. This couldn't be further from the truth. While much Christian theology necessitates a deliberate, slow pace that allows for God's work and heart to unfold over time, other instances demand swift action. Some thinking should be slow. Some thinking should be fast. The seemingly awkward dance between the quick and the slow in our relationship with God is illuminated in Exodus 12 and 13 as God delivers Israel from centuries of bondage in Egypt.

Preparing Israel for their liberation, God instructs his people to refrain from adding yeast to their bread dough. Why? God knows what is to come. He knows that their liberation from slavery will take place in one evening. There won't be time for the bread to rise. Deliverance was at hand. Israel didn't have time to sit around and wait for yeast to rise. Exodus reads,

> With the dough the Israelites had brought from Egypt, they baked loaves of unleavened bread. The dough was without yeast because they had been driven out of Egypt and did not have time to prepare food for themselves. (12:39)

To this day this seemingly inconsequential instruction about yeast continues to be enshrined in the Jewish tradition of *matzah*. Every year, as Jews across the globe celebrate the Passover, they prepare bread without yeast as a reminder of this event. The purpose behind this culinary theology is to remind subsequent generations that God's deliverance is imminently breaking in, regardless of whatever metaphorical Egypt we may find ourselves in. As with our salvation, there's simply no time to wait. God is bringing *us* home as well. It is with this sense of urgency that Israel was required to make their preparations for leaving their oppression.

Similarly, the desert narrative in Numbers reflects an overlapping theme. Israel faces repeated tests and failures, often showing a tendency to quickly forget and disobey God and his word. The Psalms emphasize the need for prompt obedience in response:

> Today, if only you would hear his voice,
> "Do not harden your hearts as you did at Meribah."
> (95:7–8)

Later, New Testament writers would often return to this potent psalm as a way to invite the follower of Christ to willingly obey God at his word—whenever, wherever, and however it is revealed. The author of the letter to the Hebrews, for instance, urges all who seek to know and be known by God to promptly turn to the Lord by hearing and obeying his voice. This same author, incidentally, quotes the text of Psalm 95:7–8 *twice* in one single chapter to make their point (see Heb. 3:7–11, 15). The author is making this command, urging us to do it without delay: Return to your God. Now. At this moment. Don't wait. So long as it is called "today." Clearly, a deep love for God should always seek to obey God's voice whenever he speaks, with an unhesitant immediacy. Such urgency should be cultivated by any person who seeks to know and love God.

But not all aspects of the Christian journey require this kind of urgency. Returning once again to the story of Israel's deliverance from Egypt, the chapter of Exodus following the first Passover finds Israel in the desert, journeying toward Mount Sinai. During this time, we are told,

> When Pharaoh let the people go, God did not lead them on the road through the Philistine country, though that was shorter. (Exod. 13:17)

Notice something interesting about God's directional leading in this passage? He very well could've taken Israel along the quickest, most expedient way. But God doesn't usher them along this route. God takes them the long way. The contrast between Exodus 12 and 13 is instructive. Israel was to leave Egypt quickly. But the road to the promised land would be very, very slow. Freedom from four hundred years of slavery may have occurred overnight. But the journey to the promised land, a short seventy-five miles or so, would take the space of some forty years. Freedom happened quickly, but the journey of salvation spanned a lifetime.

This lesson is beautifully illustrated in a story from ancient Jewish folklore. A certain rabbi was walking along a road to a city and saw a young boy at the crossroads. The rabbi asked the boy, "What is the best path to reach the city?" The boy replied, pointing, "This path is short but long, and that path is long but short." The rabbi decided to take the first path that was "short but long." As he got close to the city, he realized the road was blocked by some of the gardens and orchards that surrounded the city. He could not figure out how to get to the city gates, so he turned back and met the boy again at the crossroads. He said, "My son, didn't you tell me this was short?" The boy quickly replied, "And didn't I also say it was long?" This tale cleverly teaches that looks can be deceiving. We can all be tempted by the allure of immediacy. But sometimes the long way is indeed the best way. The rabbi learned the hard way that "the long path is short[er]."[1]

The Christian life is rhythmically slow and fast at different moments. The delicate balance is illustrated by the work of a five-star chef. Mastering the culinary arts requires years of dedication, training, and experience, not to mention the pursuit of the finest ingredients. A top-rated chef spends countless hours sourcing the freshest and most flavorful ingredients for their dishes. Yet the actual act of cooking can take mere minutes. Without perfect attention at the critical moments, all that preparation can be wasted. This intricate dance between patient preparation and precise, swift execution is challenging to master, and few ever achieve it.

Israel would have to struggle for years to finally arrive at the promised land. But this extended journey would commence on a single night of divine intervention. Why does this matter? When God speaks, we should desire to obey immediately. But it takes years of preparation to become the kind of person who desires to do God's will. This preparation involves years of submission to the biblical text, being part of a community under God's Word, performing small and great acts of obedience, and gradually becoming someone inclined to listen to and obey what the Spirit says to us. God speaks, but being ready to obey requires arduous, painstaking discipleship—the slow and deliberate work of spiritual formation. Acts of radical, spontaneous, and immediate obedience to God often come only after years of slowly, intently, and patiently being formed by God's work in our lives.

Learning how to discern when to act swiftly and when to proceed with deliberation is an art that takes a lifetime to master. We must promptly obey when God speaks, accept correction with humility, repent of sin, listen attentively, speak truthfully, cultivate humility, embody the character of Christ, and love our neighbors wholeheartedly. Conversely, we should exercise caution in doubting God's goodness; instead, we ought to be resisting disbelief in Scripture's revelations about God, heeding the Holy Spirit's guidance, respecting long-standing convictions of the church held since the apostolic era, and persevering in the ongoing work of repentance. Similar to the finesse of a five-star chef, following Jesus requires skillfully discerning when to allow slow processes their due time and when to execute swift actions decisively.

Sabbath Thinking

Loving God requires a deliberate cultivation of the kind of character that heeds his voice promptly when he calls. Regrettably, our current cultural climate is hostile to this kind of spiritual formation. Any youth pastor or undergraduate professor in the Western hemisphere understands that. In a world where students rush through life, cramming their schedules, responding to every notification, and keeping up with endless streams of new content, our hearts and minds struggle to focus when God seeks to communicate with us. Too often, we try to "run the race" (see 1 Cor. 9:24)—as Paul would call it—by going at the world's pace rather than God's pace. Becoming the kinds of people who can hear and obey God's voice requires a lifetime of training, practice, and restraint.

The biblical practice of Sabbath rest can help us begin to run this race at the pace that God desires. What exactly does the Sabbath entail? In short, it is God's blessing of a day each week that is set aside for cessation, reflection, and enjoyment of God, one another, and his creation. Set apart by God as holy at creation, the Sabbath day invites all of creation to pause, breathe, and reconnect with their Maker. Thankfully, the Sabbath and its significance is being reconsidered in a fresh way in the modern church.[2] Regular observance of the Sabbath not only benefits our physical bodies, relationships, families, churches, and the entire created order but also enriches the ways in which we think and reflect on God.

But what if the Sabbath actually helps us rethink how we reflect on God? As educators, we've learned by years of classroom experience that our students come into their studies having to navigate a chaotic set of complications and real-world challenges. Many of these students juggle excessive work hours, a burdensome amount of homework, constant digital communications, and the complexities of interpersonal relationships throughout their week. Today's students are frazzled with burdens. This leaves them overworked and fatigued—and they bring this into their education. In 2019, communications scholar Heather Day Thompson captured in a social media post something she'd observed in her students:

> I had a student once who entered college with a 1.2 GPA. She finished w/ honors, & a full ride scholarship to her next school. She was the same person she was in high school, only difference was that in college, for the first time in her life: She had a bed.[3]

Day's tweet clearly touched a nerve, almost instantaneously going viral and being shared by tens of thousands. The truth is, most of our students come to the classroom exhausted. Others, sadly, don't even have a bed to sleep on. A lack of rest certainly impacts one's education. How much more does it shape our ability to think about complex, nuanced, and mysterious matters relating to God? Even with adequate rest it's difficult to delve into the intricate narrative structure of Genesis, Paul's theology of the church, or the way Revelation addresses how Christians must engage with the powers of the age. Without rest, we tend to do the work of thinking about God by cutting corners, rushing through hurriedly, and committing the ultimate sin of seeking easy, trite, and cookie-cutter theological answers.

Frenzied minds have little room for reflection, pondering, or long-term thoughtfulness. We all know this. We are holistic creatures, and it remains nearly impossible to wall off parts of our life from other parts. Everything is downwind from everything else. When we are rushed on our way to work, we will come to work with a rushed spirit. When we come home with anxiety, we enter the living room anxious. As we return from a silent retreat with God, we bear the peace we've found into our relationships back home. Life soon teaches us that the tempo or rhythm at which one engages in one given activity can significantly influence the quality of reflection or work in subsequent tasks that one undertakes. The pace of one activity carries over into the next. This phenomenon, which has been termed by social scientists as "cognitive load carry-over," illuminates how the mental busyness of life bleeds into everything else we do. You can take a person out of rush hour, but it often takes some time to leave rush hour behind.[4]

Why is this significant? It is unrealistic to anticipate that students will enter class and calmly reflect on the profound words of Scripture when their lives are consumed by the relentless pace of modern demands. Individuals deprived of rest and conditioned to seek instant gratification often struggle to cultivate the patience required to wait on God. Furthermore, the tempo of our daily lives often carries over into our spiritual lives. If we frantically go from one activity to another all day long, we should not be surprised to discover that we struggle to pore over the words of Esther or the Psalms or biblical poetry.

Our frenetic pace undeniably broadens the impact that practicing a Sabbath has in our lives. Not only is it good for our bodies, emotions, and relationships; it also enables us to enter into the gentle, meditative space of the Holy Spirit. The still, small voice we're commanded to heed often cannot be heard in the loud, large lives we inhabit. Observing the Sabbath is more than merely taking a day off; the goal is to intentionally develop the capacity to hear, listen to, and patiently wait on God's voice. Sabbath-keeping is, fundamentally, about cultivating a disposition that enables obedience to God.

What if the problem for many of us is not that we need to read the Bible more? What if our problem is that we are cultivating a lifestyle and a rhythm that keep us from hearing God's voice even when we *do* read Scripture? Silence, solitude, introspection, grappling with questions, embracing discomfort, observing Sabbath rest, and learning to wait patiently aren't the things we *add* to reading the Bible. They are the practices we do so that we can hear God in the Bible. These are the disciplines that teach us to receive the presence of God.

Much of the ancient Jewish tradition passed down through the ages underscores the wisdom and power of waiting patiently to receive from God. One writing, the *Pirkei Avot*, advises that one begin studying Scripture at age five, delve into commentaries at ten, and pursue deep understanding (*binah*) only around the age of forty. Similarly, young men were traditionally kept from reading Song of Songs until they reached sixteen, when they were deemed better prepared for its content. Within Jewish mystical teachings such as kabbalah, access to certain texts was restricted until the age of forty, acknowledging that wisdom and life experience are necessary to comprehend life's deeper mysteries. There were age limits on when one could read certain things.[5] Not because people were illiterate but rather because they had to become the kinds of people who could handle what they read.

People who have learned to slow down have learned how to receive from God. One of the benefits of observing the Sabbath is that it prepares us to be truly present with God. This practice underscores a fundamental truth: We most deeply cherish what we are willing to pause and contemplate. Unfortunately, tech companies have recognized this aspect of human behavior and used it against us. The algorithms on our devices meticulously track what we linger on, zoom in to observe, and explore. These moments of hesitation in our scrolling unveil our innermost desires. Whether it is admiring a beautiful person, carefully reading about a subject, or thoughtfully examining something, these actions reveal the depths of the human heart. We love and prioritize what we take the time to behold.

Theological Restraint

The grounding of much Sabbath practice is laid out in Exodus 20:8–11. In the fourth commandment, we are told that the people of God are to work six days a week. But one day—the Sabbath day—is to be a day of rest to God in which "you shall not do any work" (v. 10). This naturally invites the reader to ask, What constitutes work? Quite simply, if this commandment is read as a whole, work is defined as the chosen or assigned activity that one does during the *other* six days of a week. But the Sabbath is the one day when that work has come to an intentional pause. For the farmer who works their fields and livestock six days a week, one day is to be free of farmwork. For the person who prepares meals for others, one day is marked by ceasing from preparing meals. If someone is a pastor six days a week, their hearts need one day free from pastoring.

This holy day of rest is often when God does his deepest work within us. As scholars who study biblical literature and theology, one of the ironic challenges we face is that our work of studying the Bible and theology is what we do six days a week. This raises a difficult quandary for us. If our work is in the domain of biblical scholarship and theology—and we give six days of our week to these tasks—then do we need a day away from this work? Could it be that reading the Bible and doing theology could be work from which one needs to rest? How, then, do we approach our Sabbath days if these subjects are central to our professional lives? Paradoxically, it is crucial for us to set aside one day each week to refrain from studying the Bible or theology in academic terms. Like anyone else, we require this time to step back from our scholarly pursuits and allow God's gentle shaping to permeate our being. We set aside one day a week to stop working on the Bible so that the Bible can do its work on us. God does not desire only to be studied. He also wants to be enjoyed.

The restraint that the Sabbath requires is actually, under the surface, the cultivating of true trust in God. Just look at God's commandments to his people as they wander for forty years through the desert. As God's people slowly make their way to the promised land, God provides a substance called *manna*, translated from the Hebrew literally as, "What is it?" This sticky, gooey, bread-like substance would supernaturally be placed on the ground for Israel every morning. But there remained one critical provision: Israel was to pick up extra food on Fridays (the day of preparation) so that on Saturday (the Sabbath day) they would not be collecting the manna. Only on Fridays was extra food to be collected. Every other day the people were to collect only enough for one's family or tribe.

This imparts a fascinating lesson. By telling Israel that they were not to collect manna on the Sabbath day, it is implied that God was still sending manna on the Sabbath, the day they were not to collect any. Israel experienced a day when they could have taken more food but were not allowed to. The lesson is critical. God's people were to cultivate restraint. Few would disagree that this is a clear connection to the garden of Eden story in which humans were commanded not to eat from a tree bearing delicious fruit that had been placed in the middle of Eden. Part of being God's covenant people meant obeying him by willingly refraining from taking something for oneself that appeared good and enjoyable. Restraint was needed in the garden of Eden, and it was called for again in the desert.

Sometimes we try to take more than God wants us to have. Rather than living contentedly, we work that extra day to pad the savings account. Rather than embracing simplicity, we take, take, and take to no end. Rather than resting in our relationship with God, we want more knowledge. One of the greatest dangers of any theology is that it can be used for the wrong reasons—a good thing utilized for evil intents. Too often, the task of biblical studies and theology is done not for the purposes of formation, love of neighbor, faithfulness to Jesus, or service to the church but for power, for coercion, for gaining followers, or for appearing smart and prodigious. Theology is good. But the motivations for doing theology need to be sanctified.

The Rest That Exposes Motives

How we keep the Sabbath reveals our deepest motivations. Behind every decision is a hidden motivation of the will. This is part of human nature: We become skilled at veiling our true intentions and keeping them in the dark. And while we may act out of hidden motivations known only to us, part of the holy life is recognizing that God is aware of them all. "All a person's ways seem pure to them," the author of the Proverbs writes, "but motives are weighed by the LORD" (Prov. 16:2). While we may hide under lock and key the true motives of our hearts, the Lord always knows. The Spirit sees them. This is why an intimate relationship with sacred Scripture is crucial for all of us. God's Word—what God himself has spoken truthfully to humanity—is "sharper than any double-edged sword . . . ; it judges the thoughts and attitudes of the heart" (Heb. 4:12). Nothing is hidden from God's sight.

More important than making the right decision is increasingly inviting the Holy Spirit to scrutinize why we do what we do. Those motivations shape everything about us. Without God's voice giving them shape, we all have the capacity to do some dangerous things.

The way Jesus went about ministry reveals much about his motivations. In John 6:1–15, we see Jesus feeding the recorded crowd of five thousand men (of course, there were way more people present, including women and children) in the middle of the desert. John tells us that a little boy has brought Jesus five barley loaves and two little fish. With these, Jesus does a miracle and feeds the throngs of hungry people. Clearly, there were times when Jesus multiplied bread for the purposes of the kingdom of God.

But there were other times when Jesus did not multiply bread. Earlier in his public ministry, Jesus is taken by the Spirit into the desert to be tempted by the devil (Matt. 4). Alone, tired, and hungry (the result of having not eaten for weeks on end), the devil instructs Jesus to "tell these stones to become bread" (v. 3) so that he might satiate his hunger. And Jesus *could* have done it. There was no commandment in Scripture *against* turning stones into bread. But he doesn't. Jesus resists. He rejects the serpent's instruction. There were times when Jesus refused to make bread.

Why would Jesus willingly make bread in one instance but not in another? In his book *God's Voice Within*, Christian writer Mark Thibodeaux offers a suggestion as to why Jesus would resist the devil's instruction to do something that he would later do willingly:

> Why would Jesus resist? Making bread appears at first glance to be a good and holy thing. Bread, after all, was destined to be an important instrument in Jesus' ministry. So why did Jesus resist so vehemently? He resisted because he knew that the source of his attraction to making bread at that particular moment of his life was not of the true spirit. This holy attraction was not rooted in the stirrings of the Father and would not have drawn Jesus closer to the Father.[6]

Thibodeaux is helping us see more clearly Jesus's inner logic. When the motivation for action was one of service, love, and care for others—with a desire to carry out the Father's will—Jesus made bread. But when the act was in service of self-glorification, birthed out of impulse and a rushed spirit, and inspired by and out of obedience to the invitation of the dark one, Jesus refuses to make the bread. The difference between the feeding of the five thousand and the story of the temptation in the desert comes down to one simple thing: the motivation behind it.

Why we do what we do matters. And taking the time neces-sary to wrap our minds around our motives matters as well. Slow down. Ask the heart, Why do I want to do this? There are times when doing the miraculous isn't the right thing. Take it from the first humans: Just because you have some fruit in your hands does not mean you are doing what God wants. There is such a thing as wicked fruitfulness. There simply are times when we do good stuff for the wrong reason. God is gracious. He can still work through us when we act out of dark motivations. But as we grow into maturity—entering into Christlikeness—it is the task of the one on the way of Jesus to constantly give space to the voice of the Spirit to speak to us about why we do what we do. The lesson? Don't always make the bread.

In his article "Not by Bread Alone," Japanese theologian Kosuke Koyama invites us, like Thibodeaux, to look at Jesus's temptation in the desert. He points out that the essence of the temptation—what Koyama calls the "devil's theology"—is the doing of an act that was quick, easy, and sensational. This, the theologian wisely reminds us, is the essence of the devil's work:

> The devil's theology aims at speedy and sensational results and speedy solutions. Evil-power is speedy and sensational. Waiting, enduring and hoping do not figure in the devil's theology. . . . But Jesus Christ dislikes speedism and sensationalism. He wants to build his kingdom on his act of total self-giving.[7]

Which is why it is important even for us as biblical scholars and theologians to take a day to rest from our craft. Not only do we need a day to allow the work we have been doing for six days to set into our lives. We also need a day to allow our motivations for our work to be clarified. Often, in the quiet of the Sabbath, we experience the gentle voice of the Spirit, who reminds us why we do what we do, our false motivations for doing it, and the means by which we can return to the heart of our craft and serve the church.

The Sabbath reminds us that even our deep thinking about God needs rest. We all need a day a week to stop trying to figure God out and to simply enjoy him once again in the garden of our lives.

Cultivating Theological Patience

The modern person, when seeking to think about the great mysteries of Scripture, theology, and tradition, allows themselves less and less time to do so. Although we have increased access to information, we have decreasing space to actually process and integrate it into our thinking and living. And we experience a growing mental exhaustion to boot. The result, sadly, is too often a kind of theological and exegetical impatience. We want to iron out deep mysteries with a short YouTube explainer video. The combination of mental exhaustion, the complexity of theological mystery, and diminished time for reflection has created a church of theological nibblers who snack from video to video rather than dining with a feast of Christian history and tradition. We get along by snacking, with no time to dine.

The danger of being in a theological hurry can also be seen in early Christian history. Very early on, the church sought to understand as best it could some of the great mysteries. One of these was trying to understand the nature of Christ. Christology (the doctrine of Christ) provided some of the most difficult challenges for the early church. New Christians all over the world were, for the first time, coming face-to-face with a growing diversity of beliefs and opinions as to who the person of Jesus was.

For example, one set of beliefs argued that Jesus was a human who through faithfulness and moral perfection became the Son of God. This set of beliefs, commonly called Arianism or adoptionism, did not see Jesus as divine but as a glorified human who in essence became perfected by obedience.

Another example, on the other side, was a set of beliefs that argued that Jesus was fully divine but only seemed to be human.

This was promulgated by a group of people who have been called Docetists, from the Greek word meaning "to seem" (*dokeō*). For this group, there was little doubt about Jesus's divine identity. But there was a suspicion that Jesus wasn't truly a human. He only appeared to be one, just as a ghost appears to be a person.

The earliest Christian community—faithful to the apostolic teaching about Jesus—knew that both of these were distortions of the truth. Their formulation of the doctrine of the dual nature of Christ articulated that a true, biblical, and historical understanding of Jesus must hold that he is simultaneously both fully divine and fully human. This undermined any notion that Jesus was divine at one moment and then human at another, as though he were Superman on Monday and Clark Kent on Tuesday. Jesus was not to be understood as divine at one moment and human at another. He was, at the same exact time, human and divine. Talk about a paradox and a mystery!

Keep in mind that these debates took place in the years and decades after the ascension of Christ. As one can imagine, there was a sense that this mystery needed to be ironed out as quickly as possible. Arians and Docetists, by the way, were both rightly deemed by the church as being outside the bounds of recognizable Christian thought about Jesus. But it is when we look at the belief structure of both heresies that we learn our most important lesson. The dual nature of Christ—that Jesus is both divine and human—is a difficult mystery to receive. One could say it seems irrational. These heretical groups committed the error of trying to make this mystery more understandable and more rational. They erred by making the mystery of God more palatable to the human mind.

In church history, one of the distinguishing marks of heresy is that it most often makes perfect sense. Too often, like the Arians and the Docetists, we move too quickly to try and iron out the mysteries of God. We choose quick-fix rationalism over long-suffering trust.

But rushed thinking can often do great harm. In his book *The Quick Fix*, Jesse Singal documents how, following World War II, there was a significant shift in the West toward materialism, and this shift partially displaced philosophy and theology.[8] Consequently, the subsequent decades were marked by idealism, with a widespread belief that increasing material wealth and well-being would eradicate evil and chaos.

During this period, new thought leaders emerged in pop psychology and pseudoscience who offered quick and simple solutions to the complexities of life. As Singal notes, many of these quick-fix approaches ultimately caused harm and failed to deliver the promised utopia. The notion of a swift remedy for the human condition was fundamentally flawed. In an era of rapid acceleration, we tend to overlook scholars and experts, whose insights require time and deep engagement. Instead, we gravitate toward gurus and thought leaders who provide easily digestible answers.

As the early church waded into an increasingly diverse world where people were contorting and reshaping Christian theology, people felt pressure to give quick theological responses. But many of those theological responses turned out to be heretical. Much, if not all, of the teachings considered by the early church to be outside the bounds of orthodox belief were constructed in an effort to provide immediate, boiled-down approaches to the deepest mysteries of God. Heresy, it turns out, is often theology that's in a big hurry.

Hearing and rightly responding to God takes work and time. In the opening chapter of Revelation, Jesus speaks to John the apostle and tells him, "Write on a scroll what you see and send it to the seven churches: to Ephesus, Smyrna, Pergamum, Thyatira, Sardis, Philadelphia and Laodicea" (1:11). Even the commandment to "write on a scroll" seems unremarkable given our contemporary ability to write down anything at any time we wish. But when John received this command, it would have required him—before receiving what Christ was going to reveal to him—to go and pay exorbitant amounts of money to buy parchment, purchase a pen and ink, and find a place with a flat surface to write. All of this would have taken time. We would not have the book of Revelation were John not patient enough to do the work of getting a scroll so he could carefully receive and record the revelation from Jesus Christ.

Epiphanies Need Margin

The human mind isn't as fast as we wish it were. And we end up doing potential damage to our mind when we ask it to do tasks that it is not capable of doing. Recent research has shown, for example, that skimming materials rather than actually reading them can have long-term effects on our minds. Ziming Liu has made the case that the kind of reading common to the modern mind—requiring an immense amount of skimming to examine large amounts of content—can actually dampen the neuroconnectivity of the human brain. This kind of skimming "is characterized by browsing and scanning, keyword spotting, one-time reading, [and] non-linear reading . . . while less time is spent on in-depth reading and concentrated reading."[9]

This kind of reading, it turns out, weakens the brain's capacity to actually think in long and drawn-out arguments. We not only get impatient for deep thought; we actually begin to lose our capacity for it. In his book on the Sabbath, Rob Muthiah says that this kind of reading is "like trying to run a 10k race when you've mainly been using your legs to walk from the couch to the refrigerator. You may be able to cover the distance, but you'd find it much easier if you had been using your legs to run daily for months."[10]

To enter into the mysteries of God appropriately, we must approach them at the appropriate speed. If our lives are marked by constant rushing, then we must learn to train ourselves to slow down to enter into God's presence with a new pattern of life. The desert fathers had a practice of slowing down between meetings called *statio*. It is the ancient practice of stopping one activity before starting another, of having space to breathe in between. This simple practice of taking five minutes to breathe before the next meeting, a moment to look out the window to thank God for the birds, helps us structure our busy lives not around the tasks at hand but around the God who created us.

Jesus lived this way. In several key instances, Scripture says that Jesus woke up early—before even his own disciples—in the pre-bustling hours of the day to find the space needed for intimate times of prayer with his Father. Jesus went off to solitary places to enter into conversation with God (see, e.g., Mark 1:35). The disciples who recorded these experiences noted that he was often inaccessible and difficult to find. During these times of prayer, Jesus no doubt received his marching orders for what was to come. The space that Jesus deliberately created structured his ministry in hidden ways that we will never fully understand.

Similarly, the book of Acts gives an account of the travel itineraries of Paul and his companions as they preached the gospel throughout the Roman Empire. Finding margin structured Paul's life just as it did Jesus's. After his conversion to Christ in Acts 9, he was left blind and went without eating or drinking for three days—likely sitting in solitude as he reflected on what had just happened to him (Acts 9:8–9). He even mentions going to the arid and obscure land of Arabia for a season immediately after his dramatic experience with Jesus (Gal. 1:17–18). Luke tells us that on one of Paul's final missionary journeys, as he embarked on a journey to Assos from Troas, he declined to travel by boat. Rather than sailing, Paul made the decision to make the journey "on foot" (Acts 20:13). This nearly twenty-five-mile, rugged, isolated journey would have provided Paul with much space to reflect and be with God.

What did Paul hear or learn on that walk by foot? He must have had some encounter or revelation, given that in the next two verses of Acts 20, we are told that he makes the fateful decision to say goodbye to the Ephesian elders and travel to Rome, where he would die. Did he hear from God on this prolonged walkabout? It can be assumed that he did. The reality remains that Paul's missionary journeys were filled with countless supernatural and awe-inspiring events—but such events were often structured by long, protracted periods of slow travel and obscure spaces. "We made slow headway" and "we moved . . . with difficulty" (Acts 27:7–8) could be seen as the thesis statement of these journeys. Indeed, the Christian life is a journey. In Hebrew, it is called a *derek*—a way, road, or journey.[11] In Greek, it is called the *hodos*—the way, the road, or path.[12] And it turns out to be a slow journey.

Scripture is replete with stories and instances in which key individuals in the biblical narrative hear from (or receive direction from) God when they find themselves in a place of quiet, obscurity, or impediment. In the early chapters of Exodus, God speaks to Moses through the burning bush while he cares for flocks in the quiet region around Midian. After escaping Jezebel's pursuit, Elijah finds solace and rest with God in the wilderness. David writes many psalms while in the wilderness, seeking to escape the tyrannical hand of Saul. And it is on an isolated island called Patmos that John writes the book of Revelation.[13]

Apparently, epiphanies need margin.

What does this tell us about discipleship? We all tend to prefer being around those who don't slow down the fast pace of our lives. We hate being hindered, especially by people. As we grow in our own formation and maturity, we're learning that part of the process is embracing the frustrations of slowing down as a means by which the Holy Spirit is forming us. Paul's words to the church in Rome speak to this: "We who are strong ought to bear with the failings of the weak and not to please ourselves. Each of us should please our neighbors for their good, to build them up" (Rom. 15:1–2). Bear with the failings of the weak? Who wants that? Well, the person who wants to be formed into the image of Christ does.

Bearing with the weak has a deeply practical and formational dimension. If we desire to be like Christ, we must make it our goal to spend time with people who are not like Christ. The frictions that arise from this are often frustrating, but in the end, these frustrations can cultivate a character within us that is luminescent and breathtaking. Be intentional about incorporating time in your life for people who do not honor your need for hurry and convenience. Time and again, we've observed among those who serve as caretakers for children, the non-able-bodied, and the dying—individuals with deep and often frustrating needs—a quality that is not found among the rest of us. They are shaped by the slow, the frustrating, and the inconvenient. Their patience permeates everything they do. They embrace life at the pace it comes, not the pace they want. More often than not, we will soon find that it is the slowest among us who expose our deeply beloved idols.

Truth is, the fastest road to Christlikeness is often the slow lane. Especially in a moment when *everyone* is in the fast lane. Like Moses, Elijah, David, Paul, and even Jesus, consider the gift of slowing down as part of the narrow road that very few take (see Matt. 7:14). This is a road that anyone can take, but you will find that very few are on it.

We see this in the life of C. S. Lewis, a man who contributed some of the most important literary, theological, and apologetic Christian works of the twentieth century. Despite writing thirty books and countless articles and other publications—to say nothing of his delivered speeches—he still could have done much more. In his famous biography of Lewis, A. N. Wilson points out that much of Lewis's life was marked by caring for the needs of his adoptive mother. She would put the responsibility for shopping, cooking, and cleaning on Lewis, tasks his older brother Warnie had found ways to get out of.

Warnie's journals would later reveal a deep regret that he had not taken on more of the responsibilities himself, wondering whether, had he done this, his brother would have had much more space and time to write and change hearts and minds around the world. Had he been a greater help, Warnie wondered, how much more could Lewis have written? Of course, in true humility, Lewis considered these seeming inconveniences as part of his discipleship to Christ—tasks that would provide him space to think and ponder the deep things of life.[14]

One wonders if Lewis was able to write and think the way he did *because* he had protracted periods of simple thought and reflection. We see the same sort of thing in the life of the great Christian spiritual writer Dallas Willard. In his excellent biography, *Becoming Dallas Willard*, Gary Moon points out that Willard's childhood was marked by two things. In his hometown of Buffalo, Missouri, Willard would attend yearly revivals that took place every August. Why in August? Willard writes,

> We had revivals every August; whether God came or not. And the reason we had them was because we had the crops laid by, as we said. That is, there is nothing more you can do for them until the harvest, and the harvest was not here yet. So that's a good time to have a revival. We used to call them "protracted meetings." Because if God actually showed up you could extend it, you could protract it, make it last longer. But if he didn't [show up], you'd have a revival anyway.[15]

These revivals were matched, Moon points out, with long periods of quiet, reflective, and spacious rural living—working on the farm, caring for the animals, and plowing the fields. The combination of these two things—a yearly rededication to follow Christ every August with lots and lots of space in between to process and reflect on that decision—likely shaped Willard into the man he would become.

As we slow down to think properly about God, our thinking becomes clearer over time. Revelation may happen in a moment. This is seen in the life of Abraham. The Bible recounts only seven occasions in which God appears or speaks to Abraham (Gen. 12, 13, 15, 17, 18, 21, 22). If Abraham died at 175 years old, as Scripture tells us, this means he had a notable encounter with God every twenty-five years. The epiphanies came. But there were lots of quiet years in between. Those who have been deeply formed by God often experience very rare moments of epiphany and clarity, with years and years (even decades) of contemplation between these experiences. If we have important epiphanies, we must leave room to properly absorb these lessons so that we can integrate them into our lives. Otherwise, we'll just walk right on by.

PONDER THE MYSTERIES

Answers Aren't Always the Answer

Divine Cliff-Hangers

"If God were so good, as we say he is, then why would he permit me to struggle with this for so long?"

"I'm taking time to wrestle with what I think about sexuality; but the questions are so expansive and seemingly never-ending. Will I ever arrive at the answers?"

"Why am I burdened with such a deep desire to make sense of God's plan?"

None of these questions are far-fetched or fabricated. They are but a small sample of the real questions we've been privileged to walk through with real people in our capacities as scholars, pastors, and friends. No matter one's theological background or denominational stripe, we will all, at some point, likely need to bear to some other trusted soul the raw and gritty conundrums of human existence and the questions this life provokes. Every question matters, and every question presents its own set of difficulties. Playing the kind host to each of them is what can make us deep, resilient, and wise. As we've learned, our relationship with God is not only composed of the answers we've arrived at or have been given. We are equally shaped and formed by the questions we've allowed to come with us on our journey. Few things shape us more than the questions we spend our life pondering.

Wouldn't it be great if we were simply given simple and immediate answers to all our questions? Lord knows, it certainly would make all our lives easier if God sent us a quick note the way a friend would send us a text message. But the deepest questions do not necessarily deserve quick answers. In fact, the quick answer very well may cheapen the sacredness of a holy question. Moments like these—when we seek to understand as best we can the theological conundrums that Christians have been meditating on for centuries—actually demand from time to time that we resist the temptation to offer quick answers and shallow hot takes. Deep questions deserve deep responses, which require lots of time, energy, and toil. Sometimes, deep Christian formation is possible only when we embrace the unanswerable. To try to solve a question that has been wrestled with for thousands of years with a short tweet, YouTube clip, or pithy bumper sticker is the most dangerous and flippant of responses.

Not every question that we may ask about God can come back to us as a neat and tidy package with a pretty bow on top. We believe that the importance of creating space for unanswered or unresolved questions is modeled by the inspired Scriptures. By the time we finish reading a book of the Bible, we may find ourselves losing attention or just wishing to finish the text. But we must be disciplined to stay with the text to the end. Consider the Gospels. The four Gospels often conclude their recounting of the stories and teachings of Jesus in the most perplexing of ways.

The ending of each Gospel teaches us as much as their middle and beginning. Matthew 28, for example, recounts Jesus giving his disciples their missional instructions (called the Great Commission) to go into the world to teach, disciple, and baptize the nations unto Jesus. Following this, Matthew concludes with the comforting words of Jesus:

Surely I am with you always, to the very end of the age. (28:20)

Matthew's Gospel doesn't end with the whole world worshiping Jesus. It concludes with the promise of presence. Mark's ending is odd in its own unique way. Most New Testament scholars suspect that Mark's Gospel likely ended initially at 16:8 as the women at the tomb run away "trembling and bewildered . . . [fleeing] from the tomb. They said nothing to anyone, because they were afraid" (16:8). Luke underscores how the disciples remained in Jerusalem, "continually at the temple, praising God" (Luke 24:53). However, John concludes his biography of Jesus by telling his reader that so much more could be said about Jesus. There simply wouldn't be enough paper or books in the world to do so:

Jesus did many other things as well. If every one of them were written down, I suppose that even the whole world would not have room for the books that would be written. (John 21:25)

Indeed, much can be gathered from these odd endings. Scripture, of course, is inspired through and through—every jot and tittle, as Jesus would say (Matt. 5:18). One of the more unique features of the final sentences of many of the writings in the Bible is that they never actually finish. Or they just end incompletely. Examples abound. Lamentations, for example—that book of weeping over the destroyed Jerusalem—ties no bow on the author's suffering. There is no end to the tears at the end of the book. The scroll of 2 Chronicles—the final book in the Old Testament at the time of Christ—ends with an invitation that has yet to be received:

> Any of his people among you may go up, and may the LORD their God be with them . . . (2 Chron. 36:23)

Many scholars believe this final sentence serves as a conclusive invitation to the readers, who were likely in exile and longing to come back to their home. The proverbial ellipsis provoked the question: Will *you* (the reader) return to the temple in Jerusalem? Last, the unfinished ending becomes the distinctive mark of the parable of the prodigal son in Luke 15:11–32. After running away, the younger son has returned to the father's house. But the older brother appears to have none of it. He can't stand all the grace and mercy and parties with fattened calves that his father has thrown for his brother. The story ends unsatisfyingly, without any clear ending to the story:

> "My son," the father said, "you are always with me, and everything I have is yours. But we had to celebrate and be glad, because this brother of yours was dead and is alive again; he was lost and is found." (vv. 31–32)

Why these incomplete and unresolved endings? These unresolved endings, of course, offer an implicit invitation to the reader to enter into them. Will I continue to weep and lament with God even when our suffering has no finality? Will I be an exile who seeks to return to Jerusalem? Will I be an older brother who will learn grace and make room for the long-lost brother who had departed so long ago?

We like calling these "divine cliff-hangers." Cliff-hangers—in movies or books—can profoundly impact the observer. Hollywood has built an entire industry on them, but they go all the way back to the medieval period. The writings of the Middle Ages—like

One Thousand and One Nights—would draw their readers in by ending each episode with an incomplete storyline. English novelist Charles Dickens used this literary device in much of his narrative fiction. So powerful were Dickens's cliff-hangers, it turns out, that a crowd of six thousand anxiously gathered in the streets of New York City because they were desperate to find out how *The Old Curiosity Shop* would end.[1] One wonders if Harriet Beecher Stowe's use of the cliff-hanger in *Uncle Tom's Cabin* lent it much of its popularity for a mass readership. Each of Stowe's episodes (forty total) concludes with a cliff-hanger, inviting her readers to rapt attention and anticipation.

Scripture, it seems, offers us an array of divine cliff-hangers— especially after the Easter event. Furthermore, given that each of the Gospels has embedded within it some form of a cliff-hanger after the resurrection, it seems the divine author wants us to come out of Easter willing to enter into introspection. How will we respond to the news of the resurrection? How will we live differently in light of the death of death? How does conquering our sin change how we think and live?

There's one more divine cliff-hanger we haven't mentioned yet—and it may be the most important one for the formation of the church throughout the ages: the mysterious ending of the book of Acts. Acts features lots of fascinating adventures of the apostles, but the last few chapters of Luke's chronicles of the early church are devoted to the arrest, trials, and imprisonment of Paul (including a shipwreck and a snake bite). Paul wound up in Rome under house arrest, and Luke concludes by saying, "For two whole years Paul stayed there in his own rented house and welcomed all who came to see him. He proclaimed the kingdom of God and taught about the Lord Jesus Christ—with all boldness and without hindrance" (Acts 28:30–31). We can only imagine that Theophilus (the named original recipient of the book of Acts) probably unrolled the scroll further looking for the *real* ending of Acts.

What happened next, Luke? Did an angel break Paul out of his chains? Did the magistrates have a change of heart and release him? Did Paul go on to do more ministry and have a widespread impact on thousands of people, adding countless numbers to the church of God? Luke seems to imply that Paul was under house arrest for *only* two years, but he doesn't come right out and say what happened next. Did Paul die? Was he released? Did he stay in Rome? Maybe first-century Christian readers of Acts already knew what became of Paul, but it's always nice to read a happy ending for a bit of closure and reassurance. Luke had already penned twenty-eight long chapters. What would stop him from adding a few more to tie up loose ends? We get a clue in the last two words of Acts: *parrēsia akōlutōs* ("unhindered boldness"). Luke was rallying the church. He would not have wanted the church to focus on the wrong death. Paul wasn't the point of the story. Jesus Christ was.

What these divine cliff-hangers communicate, in part, is that God isn't done with the story. Nor are we. While the account of the resurrection may have ended, there is so much left to be done in our lives as a result of Christ's accomplished work. When we confess our sins in church gatherings, we are invited to ask forgiveness for the things we should not have done. But we also ask forgiveness for the things we have left undone. That line should catch us. There is so much undone within us that has yet to be written, fleshed out, and articulated. These incomplete endings remind us of that. They remind us that God is never done,[2] and we are continually being refashioned as a result of God's ongoing work.

Divine Incomprehensibility

These cliff-hangers also have much to say to us theologically—namely, that Scripture is not an exhaustive set of facts and truths that covers every single thing the human mind may wonder about.

Scripture, inspired as it is, intentionally leaves much out. There are many stories not told, countless details omitted. And all for good reason. The goal of the Christian life is not exhaustive theological answers. No, the goal is that we would know God himself and toil to that end—"until Christ is formed" in each and every one of us (Gal. 4:19).

The humble confidence it takes to recognize the *incompleteness* of one's theological system is actually part of a robust, historically faithful approach toward Christian theology, which has always held that God can be known and, at the same time, that one's theology will never be perfected on this side of glory. Having an incomplete theology, in other words, is not synonymous with having a wrong theology. Accepting that one has an incomplete theology demonstrates one's faith and trust that God still has more to show that person in his own time. Perhaps one of the most revealing signs of our desire for a true and right theology is that we avoid thinking there's nothing left to learn and that God has nothing more to teach us. Our work of faith in Christ should always be written in ink. It is our theology that should be done in pencil.

What does this mean? Assumptions are crucial. We must assume that the God revealed in Scripture is a God who desires to be known by humans. This God is not content with being unknown. If this were not true, why would the inspired Scriptures go to such great lengths to reveal to humans the character, nature, and mission of God for and over all creation? That we even *have* inspired Scripture implies that the one who is behind them desires to be known. This simple reality is given a resounding witness throughout Scripture. The apostle John defines eternal life in terms of knowing God and the one he sent as Jesus Christ: "Now this is eternal life: that they know you, the only true God, and Jesus Christ, whom you have sent" (John 17:3). His later letters to the churches in and around Ephesus describe how he is writing to his "dear children" so that they might "know the Father" (1 John 2:14; see also 4:8; 5:20). The apostle Paul even describes the spiritual life as one that includes "growing in the knowledge of God" (Col. 1:10). As the prophet Jeremiah writes, if we boast, it should be about one thing: "that they have the understanding to know me" (Jer. 9:24).

God wants to be known. And he *can* be known. But Scripture equally reminds us of the boundaries and limitations of the human capacity for the knowledge of God. We see this, for instance, in the Psalms. David consistently comments that the knowledge of God is far beyond his own understanding or comprehension. The knowledge of God, he writes, is wonderful. But it is "too lofty for me to attain" (Ps. 139:6). He describes the knowledge of God as having "no limit" (147:5), his thoughts as "outnumber[ing] the grains of sand" (139:18) and possessing a greatness "no one can fathom" (145:3).

The New Testament writers build on this idea by showing that any knowledge of God can happen only because God himself has made the revelation a reality. In the words of Paul, God can be known only "because God has made it plain to them" (Rom. 1:19). Even within the Trinity the Father, Son, and Spirit are described as being known because they have been revealed by one of the other members of the Trinity: "No one knows the Son except the Father, and no one knows the Father except the Son and those to whom the Son chooses to reveal him" (Matt. 11:27). Even human wisdom is critiqued as a way through which people scheme to ascertain God (1 Cor. 1:21). Indeed, the Spirit "searches all things" of God (2:10). And it is only through the Spirit that these things of God can be revealed.

Scripture reveals two distinct sides to a knowledge of God. In the realm of systematic theology, this is called the "doctrine of divine incomprehensibility." The basic idea is that God can be known but never inexhaustibly. The human mind simply cannot attain a full knowledge of something that is infinite. As the Latin church fathers would put it, *finitum non possit capere infinitum*, "the finite is not capable of grasping the infinite."[3] This idea is captured by writers in the church such as Gregory of Nyssa, who speaks of the knowledge of God as "a seeing that consists in not seeing, because that which is sought transcends all knowledge, being separated on all sides by incomprehensibility as by a kind of darkness."[4] Gregory knows that God can be seen. But it is a kind of seeing that is like "not seeing."

This particular doctrine is important, yet it is often forgotten in environments where sheer rationality and reason rule the conversation. But we forget it to our own peril. The doctrine of divine incomprehensibility guards against two dangers. On one hand, it guards against theological agnosticism, which skeptically believes that knowledge of God isn't even possible. This kind of agnosticism can be seen, for example, in the writings of John Scotus Eriugena, who famously wrote, "We do not know what God is. God Himself does not know what He is because He is not anything [i.e., not any created thing]."[5] While Eriugena is not saying that God is not a real being, he is leaning heavily in a direction that aligns with the perspective of many in our own time who would say that knowledge of God is impossible. And so, in response, there is no need whatsoever to search out divine knowledge.

It also guards against a theological arrogance that believes an exhaustive knowledge of God is a possibility. We see theological arrogance being confronted in the church when we read the works of fourth-century bishop Gregory of Nazianzus, who was widely called "the theologian." One of Gregory's deepest passions was helping Christians cultivate the right kind of attitude necessary to do the work of thinking about God. In one sermon titled the "Sermon Against the Eunomians," Gregory rails against a group of Christians who allegedly had come to believe that a Christian could actually know God better than God knew himself. Gregory passionately argues against an attitude of theological arrogance. If we come to theology with pride, we fail the task at hand.

Between theological agnosticism (that nothing can be known) and theological arrogance (that everything can be known) is the doctrine of divine incomprehensibility. Our knowledge of this doctrine is rooted in Scripture. The only way we can know that we can't know everything is because Scripture reveals that fact to us. Ironically, it is a trust in Scripture that helps us know we can't be know-it-alls.

The Christian life is one marked by a fearless, never-ending, and passionate pursuit of the knowledge of God. We never end this pursuit. Consider the example of living in an intimate relationship with someone you love dearly. Though there is relational oneness, the journey of becoming aware of who that other person actually is takes a lifetime. And you never fully arrive! But your pursuit of that person must be marked by an increased knowledge that arriving at exhaustive answers and solid conclusions may be a true impossibility. When it comes to our relationship with God, we must seek God with all of our heart, mind, and soul until we come to the end of ourselves. Then, having exhausted our own pursuit, we await God to reveal and break through as he would.

Like the prophets Ezekiel and Daniel, we come to stand at the edge of a body of water. Ezekiel stands at the edge of the Kebar River (Ezek. 1), and Daniel comes to the edge of the Tigris (Dan. 10). It is there—on the edge of their own distinctive rivers—that they receive the revelation of their visions from God. This is what the doctrine of divine incomprehensibility gives to us. It beckons us to seek God as far as human reason and rationality can. But then we must stand at the edge, knowing there is only so far we can go. We then trust that God will bring the revelation we need.

Stewarding Theological Mysteries

All prophecy, N. T. Wright has said, is a signpost leading into the fog.[6] This insight exposes a critical aspect of the mystery of God— namely, when God speaks and reveals, said revelation does not bring an end to all questions or doubt. More often, we find that

God's revelation can lead us deeper into the fog of unknowing. The point of revelation isn't necessarily to provide us with all the answers our minds desire. We have ample evidence in Scripture, in fact, of individuals and communities who experienced the sheer truth of God and yet still stumbled about with further questions, doubts, and concerns afterward. Revelation isn't primarily an answer to human questions. Rather, revelation is a disclosure of God's own self that is intended to lead us more deeply to himself.

We must remember that there are always two sides to revelation. One is the human side. Any attempt at theological reflection is the part that we humans undertake. There's the hard work of study, prayer, reflection, reading, silence, and hungry pursuit. This is an essential component of theology. But we must also recognize our inherent limits. Human efforts to know God can only go so far—just as Ezekiel and Daniel could only go so far. Despite all we can do, there still is that which we simply cannot do. To borrow from the narratives of Ezekiel and Daniel, there is an "edge" to the limits of human reason.

Countless theologians in Christian history have reminded us that the human mind alone does not have the capacity to summit the mountain of revelation. This is fleshed out, for example, in the theology of Karl Barth. In the years before World War II, Barth began to recognize the limits of human reason to "achieve" knowledge of God. For Barth, humans could not ascend to some logical or rational mountaintop to behold God. This became clear for Barth when he began to see his own theological heroes lend their support to the Third Reich. He realized that God had to come to us himself. Revelation, Barth argues, is "what human beings cannot tell themselves."[7]

In other words, God never butt-dials. No revelation is ever accidentally given. Every act of revelation is intentional. One of Barth's contemporaries, another theologian named Dietrich Bonhoeffer, believed that the church of Jesus had to be cautious not to overshare the mysteries of the church with the world around them. He

called this *disciplina arcani,* or the "secret of the discipline."[8] Close
to the end of his ministry—before being hung by the Nazis—
Bonhoeffer increasingly believed that the church would be wise
not to share the treasures of its mysteries with the unbelieving
world because the world did not have the ability to steward them
with care. One scholar points out that Bonhoeffer received this
tradition from the early church, which faced similar pressures
from the empire as he had:

> The early church did not want for anyone to be told the depths of
> the teaching of the church. Instead, the early church protected the
> mysteries of the faith through the discipline of the secret, through a
> responsible sharing of the mysteries of the faith by which it resisted
> casting the pearls of the gospel before swine.[9]

What Barth and Bonhoeffer teach us is that more important
than *having* the mysteries of God is cultivating the ability to tend to
and care for these mysteries. This is the human side of revelation.

But there is also God's side of revelation. True revelation of
God is a gift and nothing else. To simultaneously recognize the
human role in theology *and* the divine gift that it is requires that
we embrace what we would call a healthy vision of "theological
mystery." What is theological mystery? Helpful direction is given
in Paul's letter to the churches in and around Colossae:

> The mystery that has been kept hidden for ages and generations,
> but is now disclosed to the Lord's people. To them God has chosen
> to make known among the Gentiles the glorious riches of this
> mystery, which is Christ in you, the hope of glory. (Col. 1:26–27)

Paul's use of the word "mystery" (Greek, *mystērion*) is central
to Colossians, in part because Paul may be combating some of
the incipient tendencies of mystery religions that operated in the
area. These religions, it was believed, offered a means of ascending

some ladder of revelation through asceticism, bodily destruction, and intellectual privilege. Paul would have none of it. The mystery of the gospel, indeed, was "kept hidden" for a time. But now this revelation of Christ's love for the world has been disclosed.

Yet notice the tension inherent in Paul's writing. The mystery is revealed. But Paul still must write a letter to explain and expound on it. Indeed, the grace of God in Christ has been laid forth for all to see and hear. But there is still so much to say about it. This tension—that Christ is disclosed and yet not fully understood—is at the heart of what we mean by theological mystery.

Theological mystery is a posture toward theology that says we simultaneously have Christ revealed and yet must embrace the knowledge that we don't fully understand this revelation. We need to create space and room in our theology for the ongoing revelatory acts of the Spirit, who will teach us as we progress through the Christian life. The psalmist writes that God's people are to "seek his face always" (Ps. 105:4). In Christ, we have God's face. Yet we continue seeking him. The fourth-century church father Augustine would pick up on this seeking in his *Exposition of the Psalms*:

> But what is meant by seek his face always? I certainly know that it is good for me to cleave to God, but if he is always being sought, when is he ever found? . . . May we think, perhaps, that even when we do see him face to face, we shall still need to search for him, and search unendingly, because he is unendingly lovable?[10]

God reveals truth that we will never fully comprehend. This, of course, should not lead to any kind of theological agnosticism. Rather, it should propel us to endlessly seek the mysteries of God. In his book on Christian history, *Fingerprints of God*, priest Robert Farrar Capon acknowledges that Americans who hear the term "mystery" may encounter a problem because they are so used to mystery novels. Capon reminds us not to equate the two. For in a mystery novel, the mystery is always fully resolved by the end of the story.[11] Not so with Scripture or revelation from God.

This does not mean God is withholding. In fact, it is important that we distinguish between a secret and a mystery. A secret is something that someone is keeping from us. It cannot be known because it is being withheld. A mystery, on the other hand, has been given, but it is just too majestic to be fully comprehended or understood. Conrad Gempf describes the difference:

> With a secret, knowledge is being withheld—there are facts or concepts you're not given. A mystery is very different. The concepts and facts are not hidden; on the contrary, you are immersed in them and they are so thick around you that you can't see the woods for the olive trees.[12]

A secret intends to keep people out. But a mystery intends for those who are in it to keep seeking. Embracing theological mystery is so crucial for our theological formation because it guards against the controlling tendency that seeks to put God in an intellectual box. Such attempts, of course, always do great harm to our love for God. The minute we seek to control God through our ideas, we end up intellectually crucifying him all over again. As Thomas Schmidt narrates the words of Jesus in a fictional interview, "Theologians got me killed and continue to cut me. Truth is like a flower whose beauty is not improved by dissection. Theology is like gold, good in itself but dangerous to own."[13]

Indeed, theological mystery recognizes the harm that comes with seeking to control God. "Mystery," writes Diogenes Allen, "withers at the touch of force."[14] Yet at the same time, theological mystery also guards against a kind of apathy that says, "Nothing can be known of God—so why even try?" The concept of theological mystery is not intended to enable a laziness by which we neglect to seek God with all of our being. Too often, sadly, the word "mystery" can be used as an excuse not to struggle and toil to understand. The task of loving God with all of our mind must mean that we spend our life's efforts to come to the edge of our own understanding. This pursuit must never end.

But too often we never press on because the word "mystery" has come to imply that we shouldn't do the journey at all. Too often it is believed that if we will never be able to come to an exhaustive knowledge about something, the journey is not worth having. Such assumptions are born of the Enlightenment, not of the Spirit. To say that we shouldn't do theology because it's all a mystery is like saying we shouldn't do surgery because we will all die anyway. No surgery is perfect. Just like no theology is perfect. "Just because no medical procedure is perfectly sterile," writes one philosopher, "does not mean that we should do surgery in a sewer."[15] A slow theology is not a lazy theology. It is not using the mystery as an excuse to cut off our human work of seeking the knowledge of the Lord.

Synoptic Theology

G. K. Chesterton once wrote, "The riddles of God are more satisfying than the solutions of man."[16] The heart isn't looking for human-made answers to divine mysteries. We long for something deeper. Let us return to the Gospels. We have four Gospels—three of which are very similar to one another. Matthew, Mark, and Luke share many of the same stories, phrases, and details about the three-year earthly ministry of Jesus of Nazareth. New Testament scholars call these the Synoptic Gospels. We call them the Synoptics because they seem to look at the same stories of Jesus "with" (*syn*) "eyes" (*optics*). That is, while looking at the same narratives, each offers its own unique vantage point on these stories that together give us an intimate image of who Jesus actually was.

If Matthew, Mark, and Luke are the Synoptic Gospels, what do we do with John's Gospel? His account of the story of Jesus is entirely different from the Synoptics. For instance, consider the parables of Jesus. There are, in total, some thirty-eight different parables found in the teaching ministry of Jesus. Yet, notably, not one of those parables was included in John's account. Or look at the place of exorcism. While the Synoptics regularly portray Jesus casting out demons, there is not a single demonic exorcism located in John's Gospel. This does not mean that John's account was wrong. Quite the opposite—it merely means John wants to include other details that were not in the Synoptics. We see this in how John includes some stories of profound importance that are included only in his Gospel and not the Synoptics—namely, the wedding miracle in Cana (John 2) and the foot washing of the disciples (John 13).

Why these differences?

The differences between the Gospels are not problems. When a critic of the New Testament looks at these differences, they may claim that they are contradictions. But this claim reveals the bias of the one who claims it. Westerners often think that if two witnesses make two various claims, they must be contradicting each other. But that is not always true. What the world may see as a contradiction is what Christians call a paradox. These differences are not problems—they are intentional.

That the early Christian community intentionally included all four Gospels—and not just one—speaks to the fact that they not only knew there were differences but also *wanted* those differences to be included into the tapestry of Scripture. In the late second century AD, a respected Christian writer named Tatian found the differences in the four Gospels problematic. Opponents of Christianity would point out that there are "contradictions" in the Gospels, and that must mean they are not accurate or reliable. So Tatian created one "super-gospel" that is called the Diatessaron (from Greek, meaning "one document made from four texts"). Tatian's aim was to compose one coherent story about Jesus, eliminating any dissonance, confusion, or uncomfortable questions posed by readers of the four Gospels when they encountered differences. At first, many churches appreciated the editing work of Tatian—they liked the simplicity and elegance of the Diatessaron.

But several major theologians rejected the Diatessaron. Simplicity may be what we want, but it's not always what we need. Irenaeus of Lyons (ca. AD 130–202) defended what theologians call the "Fourfold Gospel"[17] by pointing to how the unique contributions of Matthew, Mark, Luke, and John are like the four angelic creatures who appear in Ezekiel 1:10: each one has four faces—the face of a man, a lion, an ox, and an eagle. Irenaeus found these creatures to be like signs pointing to the necessity of four distinct testimonies. Others supported the Fourfold Gospel as well: Hippolytus of Rome, Origen of Alexandria, Jerome, and Augustine. Matthew's Gospel was likened to the face of a man, given Matthew's genealogy account of Jesus and his identity as the Davidic Messiah. Mark was often associated with the lion, reflecting the power and majesty of Mark's Christ. Luke was the ox, as his Gospel especially dwelt on the sacrifice of Christ. And John was the eagle, indicating the "high-flying" perspective on Christ's divinity.

These theologians who opposed the Diatessaron understood that no single author or vantage point could capture the whole account, not Matthew, Mark, Luke, or John—and certainly not Tatian. Four accounts are *better* than one. That is, the more eyes that are on the situation, the more filled out the story becomes.

In *The Lord of the Rings* trilogy, the great evil Sauron has not two eyes but just one, rendering him unable to see distances or depth. Why, then, would Sauron be so neurotic about a couple of hobbits far off who are not even close to Mordor? Because with only one eye, there's no depth to his sight. Every threat is an immediate threat even if it is far off. What seems far away looks the same as something that is close.

The four sets of eyes give depth, color, and texture to the story of Jesus. Only with multiple eyes can we see the whole picture. Similarly, it would be safe to assume that the Gospel writers wanted to be able to fill in details from their experience with Jesus that were not included in the others' accounts. Again, this may explain why John's Gospel is so different and why it has been called by some the "maverick" Gospel. He isn't a renegade. John is writing his Gospel significantly later than Matthew, Mark, and Luke. And given that he has had extra time to think about and reflect on the stories of Jesus, he felt some accounts needed to be included that the others had not put in their Gospels.

The extra decades John had before writing his account means that he had more time to meditate on these stories. Why would John be the only one to include the foot-washing account? Well, because we don't tend to appreciate true service when we receive it. Nobody fully appreciates the loving care of a mother or father when they have it. Only later, upon reflection, is the significance of such care acknowledged. What if John, upon years of reflection, came to fully see what it meant for the disciples that God himself had come to wash their feet?

The fact that there are four vantage points to the person and history of Jesus can help us embrace the mystery of God as we appreciate that different approaches toward theology can help us see the bigger picture. None of us, if these accounts are instructive for us, has the final, authoritative, and ultimate picture of Jesus. In fact, so long as we are looking at the same Jesus, the *only* way that we can come to get a fuller picture of Christ is to learn to listen to one another.

Practicing the Mystery of God

Realizing that we have a role to play and that this role will never lead to an exhaustive understanding of God has so many benefits in our relationship with God. Four immediate benefits arise through this understanding. First, it helps us not to live by theological hubris. Indeed, we may know much about God. As we should. But theological mystery reminds us that there is a great deal we don't know. All our theological knowledge is preliminary—not final. Christ himself is the only final revelation of God. As followers, we are always *behind* him. Theological mystery reminds us that we will always have so much more to learn because we are unable to behold any of the mysteries perfectly.

This is why doctrines such as the Trinity are so integral to Christian orthodoxy. The Trinity simply cannot be fully understood. Even our feeble efforts at trying to explain it—through silly metaphors about eggs and water molecules—only rationalize the sacred mystery that is God's nature. These metaphors can be helpful to the degree that we do not see them as perfect. The gift of the Trinity is that it structures our life around theological humility. One cannot be prideful and receive the theology of the Trinity, because no person can conquer God's nature. "God cannot be counted," Augustine once said.[18] That is, the Trinity prevents us from beholding God arrogantly, as though we could define him.

Second, theological mystery cultivates epistemic humility, or thinking about God without a spirit of arrogance. It will be impossible for humans to ever fully plumb the depths of God. There will always be more for us to learn no matter how theologically wise we may become. Consistently entering into the mysteries of God demands that we always be over our skis, so to speak. Any person who has entered graduate school will experience this as well. As passionate as we may be, we realize before long that there is simply so much we do not know. This can be one of the most important experiences of our lives.

Augustine also demonstrated this humility in his own thinking. "If you fully understand it," he writes, "then it can't be God."[19] If it can perfectly fit into a spoon, then we've got no business whatsoever calling it the ocean. One of the greatest signs that we have wrongly done the work of theology is if our knowledge of God makes us more full of ourselves rather than more humble before God.

Third, theological mystery reveals our deep need for the Spirit of God. Whenever humans try to build something to reach God—such as the tower of Babel—God seems intent on coming to dethrone us in our pride. As humans use language to coordinate their attempt to ascend, God divides the tongues so that their plan becomes an impossibility. This story is reversed in the Pentecost story. God divided the tongues in Babel, but at Pentecost, God gives the church the ability to speak in all tongues. The many nations gathered in Acts 2 would not have understood each other previously. But by the work of the Spirit, those who could not understand each other whatsoever were now able to.

All the nations can now understand what the church is saying. This "overcomprehensibility," as theologian Michael Welker calls it, is marked by shock. "This unbelievable comprehensibility," Welker writes, "is what deeply confuses and frightens those around them."[20] The lesson of Pentecost is not that the church now has the ability to know every language and speak to every culture. That does happen and that can be the fruit of the Spirit. But the central lesson of Pentecost is to remind the church of its need and dependence on the Holy Spirit to do what the Spirit wants to do. We may do great theological work to understand how we can help bear the gospel to the world. But this is not enough. The church is powerful only as it experiences the Spirit's power.

Last, theological mystery points us toward the goal of Christlikeness. To love God is to love God for who he is, not who we wish him to be. As we enter into deeper knowledge of God, we are more deeply formed into his image. This is the sign of relational intimacy. In a marriage, intimacy is realized only to the degree that each member is known for who they actually are. Secrets, in this case, are actually what get in the way of true transformation. While God is mysterious, he withholds no secrets from us.

In fact, part of entering into Christlikeness comes by becoming increasingly aware of our humility before God. Henri Nouwen is attributed with having written, "Theological formation is the gradual and often painful discovery of God's incomprehensibility. You can be competent in many things, but you cannot be competent in God." Christlikeness entails the work of making space in our life for God to be who he is. If Christ comes to us in the incarnation, then our task is the work of hosting him.

But, as history has shown, when humans hosted God in the person of Jesus, they did so poorly. In the first century, people held expectations about who God should be were he to come. Ancient Jews did not want the Messiah to come and lay down his life as a suffering servant. Rather, they wanted a conquering savior who would annihilate the Roman Empire. Ironically, the very people who claimed to know the most about God, the theologians, were the ones who were most unable to make room for God when Jesus came to dwell among us. The theologians killed God. Why? Because theologians often love their notions of God more than God himself. We conclude with the wisdom of Nouwen:

> Someone who is filled with ideas, concepts, opinions and convictions cannot be a good host. There is no inner space to listen, no openness to discover the gift of the other. It is not difficult to see how those who "know it all" can kill a conversation and prevent an interchange of ideas. Poverty of the mind as a spiritual attitude is a growing willingness to recognize the incomprehensibility of the mystery of life.[21]

GO TO THE PROBLEMS

Challenge Yourself to Not Run
from the Difficulties

Theological Problems

During our Oregon summers, there's little I (A. J.) enjoy doing
more in the evening than sitting underneath our giant backyard
sequoia trees and taking in the glory of the glimmering stars.
Given that it rains about six hundred days a year here, it is often
the only chance an Oregonian has to see these celestial beau-
ties. This particular July day had been a hot one—and it came
at the end of a family day at the county fair. Tired legs and all, I
stretched out on our rickety Adirondack chairs, leaned back, and
took in the heavens. Almost immediately, my eyes unexpectedly
caught something. There it was: stretching out over nearly half
of the Oregon night sky, fifteen to twenty distinct lights—looking
almost as stars—silently followed each other across the twilight

horizon. There was no sound. For nearly thirty seconds, I sat, dumbfounded, jaw dropped, at what I was seeing.

I sprang to action. Pulling out my phone, I managed to snap a few hasty photos of the moving objects. But I wanted others to see them too. So I ran inside as quickly as I could to bring out my wife and son to confirm the sighting. Standing together on our back deck, we saw something none of us ever thought we'd see: UFOs. All too soon, my son became understandably afraid. My wife—the wise mother—sensed his anxiety and whisked him inside to assure him all was well. And I stayed outside transfixed at the sight.

The lights soon fell out of sight. As they stretched into the distant horizon over our home, my experience was coming to a close. I rushed inside and found my computer. I was soon scouring my social media sites to try and see if anyone else in my neighborhood had just seen what we had seen. Indeed, I was not alone. Others began sharing their images and experiences. I shared mine. Before long, there was a small but committed group of people convinced they'd just seen extraterrestrials.

In all honesty, the moment presented a particular kind of crisis for me—particularly as a theologian. Some of my theological passions are in the areas of ecological theology, the church, mission, ethics, doubt, and the Holy Spirit. But very little of my theological energies had gone to exploring the realities of UFOs or extraterrestrial life. Over the years, I've heard some fringe theological lectures on the topic and taken in some of my students' stories. Long ago, I read C. S. Lewis's fictional Space Trilogy series that outlined his otherworldly vision. But these were more novelties than anything. I'd never actually had to think about the reality of aliens or UFOs because I'd never experienced either—that I knew of. In short, this experience of mine did not align with my theology. Given that I'd never really thought all that much about the topic, or really believed they existed, my experience did not have any theological categories.

By morning's light, we discovered that these lights were nothing more than a string of Starlink satellites. Everyone in our family was relieved. Still, moments like these represent a critical part of the spiritual life: moments that present what have been called "theological problems." As I stood, staring into the sky, nearly everything I thought I believed was being demolished in a few short seconds. Every follower of Jesus has experienced, or will experience, these theological problems. They can come in many forms:

1. A deeply held theological conviction turns out, on further study, to be different from what is found in Scripture. In this theological problem, we discover that our theology falls short of the biblical storyline. We are then forced to ask, Do we believe our theology or the Scriptures?

2. What the Bible describes is the nature of the universe is not *our* experience of the universe. And we are left wondering if the Bible is actually true.

3. An experience we've had shows us that our theological beliefs do not have the capacity to contain said experience. Such as seeing what appear to be UFOs in your backyard skyline when you'd never developed any theological containers for extraterrestrials.

As one can tell, this is exactly what was taking place in my backyard. The problem was not the experience I was having. I was definitely having that experience. It was real. I have the photos. The problem was that I had never developed any kind of theological container to help me understand such an experience. Which is why experience can be so profoundly important for our theological journeys. Our experience can often shape our theology more than our theology shapes our experience—for better or worse. When it comes down to it, for good or bad, humans are prone to believe what our eyes see more than what books tell us to believe.

We might define a theological problem as a moment in which reality as we are experiencing it does not fit into, align with, or correspond to one's current knowledge, theology, or perception of reality. In general, for the Christian, there are three triangulated realities that shape who we are and who we are becoming: the Bible, our theological beliefs, and our experience. When two or three of these do not align with one another, we are facing a theological problem.

This is the heart of what this book is all about: how to walk through these questions faithfully. Every follower of Jesus will confront theological problems in their journey with Christ. The question is not *if* we will experience them but rather *how* will we walk through them well. Sadly, when many Christians confront theological problems, their first response is to discount the voice of the Bible. A great example of this in higher education settings is when students who love the Bible are asked to come to terms with scientific knowledge in a post-Darwin era. In their Bible class, they are taught that God is the Creator of all. But in their biology course, they are learning that the earth is far older than they may have been taught as children.

What that student is experiencing is a very real theological problem. What will they listen to? The teaching of Scripture or the teaching of their biology professor? Too many, it seems, believe they should plug their ears to science and listen solely to the Bible (what we call "fundamentalism"). In seeking to resolve the theological problem of creation, some have made the case that science must be wrong—or, in worse cases, the work of the devil. But this makes a fatal error by assuming that God created a world marked by lies and deception. In fact, when I (A. J.) was a brand-new Christian, I was told that God had placed dinosaur bones in the ground to test our faith. This made little sense. Why would a God who died on the cross for me spend his time trying to pump-fake me into hell? Certainly God would not do this.

Others resolve this theological tension by arguing that we should ignore the Bible and only trust science (what we would call "scientism"). Even some of our biblical scholars have made this case. In a famous essay titled "The Theological Problem of the Old Testament Doctrine of Creation," Old Testament scholar Gerhard von Rad argues, in essence, that the point of the creation story in the Bible is not about creation itself as much as it is a prologue to the story of salvation.[1] In short, in this misplaced step, von Rad makes the assumption that the Bible has little to nothing to say about the nonhuman creation. A move like this is seductive when we face theological problems because it alleviates the pressure from the biblical side.

But we are convinced there is a better way to navigate theological problems. The question is how.

Case Study: Asaph and Psalm 73

An interesting case study of how to navigate a biblical or theological problem can be seen in Psalm 73. Eleven of the psalms in the psalter are attributed to a character named Asaph. Little is known of him other than he was a prominent Levitical singer and prophet who took his seat in King David's court. His lineage was significant as well: his descendants, the sons of Asaph, served as a prominent family guild of temple musicians in ancient Israel. The psalm itself is the first of eleven psalms that are explicitly connected to the character of Asaph from Psalms 50 and 73–83.

Psalm 73 is unlike other psalms. While some of the psalms (such as Ps. 1) are about the "blessed life" and others are about a life of praise before God, this psalm has a more sour note to it. Psalm 73 is broadly considered a "wisdom psalm" with a bent toward sadness and grief. The author expresses frustration with God about the way that life is going. There seem to be three core complaints that are centered in this song.

First, in verses 1–2, Israel seems to be doing phenomenally well—whereas the author is not. "Surely God is good to Israel, to those who are pure in heart," the author writes. "But as for me . . ." That "but as for me" gives voice to what the author is experiencing. Asaph seems to be saying that as he looks at all of God's people, they appear to be thriving. The people of God are doing great. But as Asaph looks at his own life he sees something quite different. In our own contemporary context, this would be tantamount to seeing that every other person who is seeking to follow Jesus appears on the outside to be happy, doing well, and taken care of, all the while we are increasingly frustrated with the way our life is going.

Second, the author is experiencing a heavy dose of what has been called the "envy of the wicked."[2] When the author looks at those who have not loved God or sought his ways, they see people who appear to be doing well, making good money, and leading an exceedingly happy life. This creates a problem. Because to love God doesn't always lead to a better bottom line, a fitter body, or a life of exceeding happiness. Rather, a life with God can lead to *more* pain and difficulty. In short, the envy of the wicked is the jealousy the righteous have for the joy, happiness, and success the wicked seem to be enjoying. This unsettling emotion leads us to believe that those who couldn't care less about God are doing much better than those who do love God.

Third, this has led to Asaph's general sense that everyone who has little regard for the Lord is seemingly blessed, while the author himself is not. When I teach this, I refer to it as the "prosperity gospel in reverse." If the prosperity gospel is the belief that through faith in Yahweh we will be given all the prosperity our hearts desire, then this envy of the wicked is the belief that believing in Yahweh has not blessed me and has even diminished me in a world where everyone else seems to be killing it.

These are undeniably powerful emotions. And the author is confronting them head-on. What we are observing is a great example of a theological problem. The author knows God is good and that God blesses him and loves him—but why, when he looks at his life, does this not appear to be the case? Why do those who are far from God and have no interest in seeking him have all the joy, happiness, and freedom? That is often what many of our theological problems are: frustration that our faith is not giving us what we think we should have coming to us.

Scripture is so emotionally transparent. It's a marvel that the words are actually included in Scripture, a fact that is instructive. That we even have this psalm in the Old Testament—inspired and canonized into the text—should teach us a great deal about how we navigate our own theological problems. Notice, first, that the reality of a theological problem in the heart of a covenant person is intentionally included in the biblical canon. God, it appears, does not hide from us the reality of difficulties in our theology. If God's Word is inspired, as we believe it is, this speaks to the fact that the God of the Bible is the kind of God who does not deal in sleight of hand, gaslighting, or deception. The very presence of Psalm 73 speaks mightily to the Bible's honesty about the challenges of thinking well about God.

This psalm would have been traditionally sung in a community of worship. This isn't just someone's journal entry hidden from everyone's sight. This psalm would be sung by the people of God in synagogue services, temple services, and the like. In modern times, one of the signs of injustice is when an organization goes into impression-management mode—seeking to control what people think about the organization rather than being an organization that actually seeks to be good.[3] What is most interesting is that the psalm does not in the slightest seek to manage our impressions of what life with God is actually like. That this was to be sung—together, mind you—speaks not only to the fact that theological problems are a normative part of life with God. They are also meant to be wrestled with as a community.

By the time we finish the song, we see that there is no clean and neat resolution to these theological problems. Rather, the resolution is not in what we may want or what we think it *should* be. There is no answer to the theological problem that the psalmist is facing in Psalm 73. Three times the author says "surely." This has often been called Asaph's "sanctuary experience." Something has changed for Asaph. It's not that he has his answer. No. Rather, he has seen God. By the end of the psalm, Asaph says, "But as for me, it is good to be near God. I have made the Sovereign LORD my refuge" (v. 28). Asaph doesn't have a perfect answer to his theological questions. Asaph has a perfect God who is with him as he ponders those questions.

Learning to Read the Bible to Be Known by God, Not Just to Know God

There are a lot of Bible study tools out there that are helpful and good, but in order for God to speak to us and shape us in all the ways he wants to, we have to really understand *why* we read and study Scripture. There is a widespread assumption that the goal of Bible study is *knowledge*. Knowledge is important, of course. Dr. Seuss once wrote, "The more that you read, the more things you will know. The more that you learn, the more places you'll go."[4] Humans are designed to be hungry for learning, to better understand the world around them, to explore, to study, and to thrive. Overall, knowledge is good. But the Bible differentiates between two kinds of knowledge when it comes to how we relate to God, one good and one bad. There is a kind of pursuit of information and knowledge that makes us (seemingly) more *independent* from God, acquiring power through insight that gains us what we think is autonomy.

We see this, for example, in the garden of Eden. Eve and Adam wanted to eat from the tree of the knowledge of good and evil when the serpent told them that "you will be like God, *knowing* good and evil" (Gen. 3:5). It wasn't enough to trust in God's commands and take him at his word. They wanted to fully know *for themselves*, and this kind of knowledge sowed a seed of doubt in their relationship with God. In that moment of history, humans decided that it was more important to know about God than to actually love God. We might call this bad kind of knowledge "separating knowledge." This is essentially a self-centered form of learning, collecting information for *oneself* rather than focusing on growing closer to God.

The Bible clues us into a second form of learning that is the opposite of separating knowledge, one that is determined to know God more intimately. Theologian Kevin J. Vanhoozer has popularized the purpose of opening Scripture as simply "reading to know God."[5] Vanhoozer points to this second type of knowledge, which we might call "binding knowledge," the kind of knowing that opens your soul to another and forms a bond, in this case with the triune God.

We see a clear distinction between these two kinds of knowledge in Paul's instruction to the Corinthians. Paul wrote his first (canonical) letter to these believers in Corinth primarily in order to combat cataclysmic misunderstandings about who God is, the power of the cross, and how Christians should live in community. Today, we benefit greatly from Paul's corrective teaching, but when he wrote this lengthy epistle, he was deeply pained by how far this Christian community had strayed from the truth of the gospel and the blessed way of Jesus Christ. A lot of their errors had to do with misunderstanding the differences between these two kinds of knowledge.

In 1 Corinthians 8, Paul addresses a particular practical issue in the Corinthian church, but it reflects a major theological misunderstanding. Some Christians were eating meat that had been used in a sacrificial ritual dedicated to idols. They claimed that this was not engaging in idolatry because there is only one true God. But they did not take seriously that this might be a stumbling block to some believers who might be tempted to fall back into idolatry. Paul takes the time to unpack deeper theological issues at the heart of this problem. Some Corinthians were abiding by a pseudospiritual motto, "We all possess knowledge" (1 Cor. 8:1), which basically amounted to, "I know a lot, and I know I'm right." That's the kind of *separating* knowledge that got Adam and Eve into hot water. These Corinthians were not caring for their fellow believers; they were clinging to privileged knowledge and were proud of their intellectual superiority. But Paul called them out on it: "Knowledge puffs up while love builds up" (v. 1). Some kinds of knowledge inflate our egos, but genuine Christian thinking should lead to good things not only for oneself but also for the other.

Another Corinthian slogan was "I have the right to do any-thing!" This was their way of expressing "Christian freedom." Again, Paul was quick to fire back: "But not everything is bene-ficial" (6:12) and "Not everything is constructive" (10:23). That word "constructive" (Greek *oikodomeō*) refers to building up something (like a house), making it steady and strong. Genuine Christian knowledge is not an isolating or separating knowledge; it is a *binding* knowledge.

At one point in the letter Paul gets down and dirty: "Those who think they know something do not yet know as they ought to know" (8:2). Paul was saying something like this: "Doubling down on separating, ego-inflating knowledge will not bring you closer to God, closer to wisdom, or closer to the truth. It will push you further and further away." Instead, "whoever loves God is known by God" (8:3). Notice the clever switch that Paul makes here. The most important spiritual goal of the Christian life is not to seek perfect knowledge but rather to seek to be fully known by God. But wait, doesn't God know everything? This is where Paul makes a clear distinction between mere informational knowledge and the surpassing value of relational knowledge. The latter is the better path, the one that Adam and Eve should have taken, and it is not about collecting knowledge for oneself; it is about drawing closer to another through a deeper knowing of the other, in this case God. Time and time again, Paul expresses this in terms of love. Love of God is why we read Scripture and why we turn to him for wisdom and truth. Yes, the Bible is full of true information about creation, the history of Israel, the story of Jesus, and the life of the early church—but to what end? To the end of loving God, of knowing him personally and opening ourselves up to be known by him.

Overthrowing the "Tyranny of Lust"

One of the church's most important teachings on this topic is Augustine's book *On Christian Doctrine*. He begins by establishing the proper way to interpret Scripture. In his corpus of writings, Augustine established that the brokenness of sin means that human passions and desires and loves are misshapen and misguided; the formative work of God is precisely to reshape the heart and to order our loves rightly in order to become the creatures we were always meant to be. Thus, it is no surprise that in *On Christian Doctrine*, Augustine repeatedly instructs that the goal of reading Scripture is to have the "law of love" written on our hearts, the dual commands expressed in Matthew 22:37, 39: "Love the Lord your God with all your heart and with all your soul and with all your mind" and "Love your neighbor as yourself." When we read *any* part of the Bible, then, we ought to recognize that God's Word is always pointing toward that end; in other words, love is the fulfillment of God's instruction.[6]

Augustine went as far as to say that even if you don't quite understand what a passage from Scripture means, or if you happen to get the interpretation wrong, as long as your heart and life are moved to love God and neighbor, you have done right by the gospel and by Christ. Augustine explains it this way: Imagine you are trying to get somewhere on the highway but you take the wrong exit. As long as the detour gets you to the final destination *eventually*, no harm is done. Augustine believed that if your communion with God was genuinely focused on faith, hope, and love, then even if you didn't have a Bible anymore, you'd still be able to worship and serve God sincerely. Augustine was not discouraging believers of his time from reading their Bibles. On the contrary, he was trying to focus their devotion on ever-deeper intimacy with God.[7]

Too often, we read Scripture to check a box on our religion list or to mine the Bible for information or to please a spiritual friend or leader. There can be many benefits from reading the Bible, but Augustine is correct that there is only one ultimate purpose: to grow closer to our Lord. This resonates with a poem written by an English bishop named Richard de Wyche:

> Thanks be to thee, my Lord Jesus Christ,
> for all the benefits thou hast given me,
> for all the pains and insults thou hast borne for me.
> O most merciful redeemer, friend, and brother,
> may I know thee more clearly,
> love thee more dearly,
> and follow thee more nearly, day by day.
> Amen.[8]

Though Augustine lived a millennium before de Wyche, no doubt he would have approved. Scripture reading is about worship, and worship is about learning to love the Lord more dearly, day by day. (And if you're wondering if this poem inspired the *Godspell* musical number "Day by Day," you'd be right.)

What Augustine and de Wyche endorse is a certain mindset when we approach Scripture—one we should consider for our own lives. Are we reading it as the possibly fallible words of mortals that must be scrutinized and questioned, or are we reading it as divine revelation given to us for our formation and benefit, to draw us closer to God? Skeptical academic interpreters of the Bible often employ what's called a "hermeneutic of suspicion," where they seek to look beneath the surface of the text to discover problematic hidden ideologies and power structures that have shaped the values and directives. There are some benefits that can come from utilizing historical, social, and philosophical tools used by academics, but someone who reads the Bible to know God and follow Christ will not produce fruit using such a thoroughgoing skeptical posture.

This way of reading is helpfully discussed by renowned biblical scholar Richard Hays in a *Christian Century* article titled "Salvation by Trust? Reading the Bible Faithfully."[9] Hays begins with first principles of knowing and being. When we come to God, we are in no position to question him; rather, we humbly seek to have truth and life revealed to us *by* our Creator and Redeemer. The modern academy, Hays warns, often represents the biblical writers as little more than "oppressive promulgators of abusive images of God." They tell us that the Bible is bad for us, bringing forward from ancient history all kinds of sexism, racism, and xenophobia. Hays is sympathetic to concerns that the Bible could be used to promote violence or hatred. But Christians from the beginning have believed that the Bible was given by God (through humans) to point us to truth, the good news of salvation in Jesus Christ, and the way of faith, hope, and love.

There is room, Hays explains, for a critical hermeneutic where we know not to imitate everything in the Bible (just as we now repudiate the institution of slavery, which was common in biblical times), but overall Christians must be guided by a "hermeneutic of trust." He chooses this word "trust" as a helpful rendering of the Greek word *pistis*, which is usually translated "faith." There is a long tradition in English of translating *pistis* as "faith," but Hays argues that when used for how we relate to God, it is better understood as "trust," as in a relational commitment. Mortals are sometimes *not* trustworthy, but God is always trustworthy. Hays points to the example of Abraham, who was praised by Paul in Romans 4:18–21:

> Against all hope, Abraham in hope believed and so became the father of many nations, just as it had been said to him, "So shall your offspring be." Without weakening in his faith, he faced the fact that his body was as good as dead—since he was about a hundred years old—and that Sarah's womb was also dead. Yet he did not waver through unbelief regarding the promise of God, but

was strengthened in his faith and gave glory to God, being fully
persuaded that God had power to do what he had promised.

Abraham "believed" (or "trusted") God's promise, despite the
seeming impossibility of producing children in his old age. Abraham had every right, according to human logic and experience,
to be skeptical or suspicious, but instead he clung tightly to God's
message. According to Hays, "Thus, Abraham becomes the proto-
type of the community of faith, which interprets all human experience through trust in God's word. In short, Abraham exemplifies
a hermeneutic of consent, a hermeneutic of trust."[10] Hays refers
to this also as a hermeneutic of "death and resurrection," a way
of seeing God and the world through a gospel lens. We must die
to our skepticism and doubts and allow our trust and assurance
to be based on the truth of the resurrection life of Jesus Christ.
Scripture and our understanding of the world from mere human
knowledge are not always going to line up. Where do we place the
greater authority? On our personal knowledge, which will lead to
skepticism, doubt, and distance from God, or on God's revelation,
which can then shape how we see the world?

Hays offers three entailments of adopting a "hermeneutic of
trust." First, worshiping God through Scripture reading requires
a posture of trust. Like Paul, we too must approach God humbly
and with open hands. Second, there is indeed a place for suspicion but not toward God. Rather, suspicion should be directed
toward ourselves because we are flawed and often misguided
people. As Hays affirms, "Our minds must be transformed by
grace, and that happens nowhere more powerfully than through
reading scripture receptively and trustingly with the aid of the
Holy Spirit."[11]

Finally, Hays proposes that the true work of biblical study is
actually *hearing* the text. We must patiently and perceptively tune
into the frequency of God's communication to us in such a way
that it cultivates and promotes trust. Read the Bible, Hays advises,

in such a way that you love the text more and more because you discover the gospel and the God who loves us in that gospel.

Which brings us back to Augustine. If we are reading the Bible rightly and well, it is like a recharging machine for the vitality of our lives, as long as we are applying this kind of hermeneutic of trust in God. We live under the burden of sinful desires and the domination of the flesh, and the only way to be liberated fully and finally from that is to cast out the old master of sin and welcome the rule of Christ. Augustine calls this the "tyranny of lust" and the final "reign of love."[12] Keep meditating on the text of Scripture, Augustine advises. Mull over the Word of God again and again and again until love of God and love of neighbor has completely overwhelmed you.

Problems vs. Tensions

When we encounter theological problems—especially when we find difficult things in Scripture—we must remember that not all problems are meant to be solved. Some problems are intentional and are to remain. We call these "tensions." Marcion of Sinope (AD 85–160) was an early Christian theologian who came to believe strongly that the Old and New Testaments could not be theologically reconciled, that the New Testament alone reflected the true gospel, and furthermore that even the New Testament that was passed around in his time had been altered and corrupted from its original form. We know that Marcion wrote several works, but none of them have survived. We do have extensive refutations from other early Christian theologians such as Justin Martyr and Tertullian. From these polemical works (such as *Against Marcion*), we have come to learn that Marcion tried to reconstruct a hypothetical original set of apostolic writings free from what he considered later additions that form a more pro-Judaism bent. For example, Marcion cut out most of the references to Abraham in Galatians (e.g., Gal. 3:6, 7, 14, 16, 18, 29). It was unfathomable to Marcion that the holy apostle Paul would favorably refer to the Old Testament patriarch Abraham.

Marcion's major theological concerns with the Old Testament were laid out in a work he wrote titled *Antithesis*. Again, this work hasn't survived, but from what other ancient writers have said about it, we know the gist of what he wrote. First, Marcion was convinced that if dualities exist in the world (such as light and darkness), and the Old Testament God says "I . . . create evil" (Isa. 45:7 KJV), then there must be *another* God who is pure goodness. Thus, Marcion differentiated between the "Creator God" (Yahweh), who is essentially evil, and the "Supreme God" (Jesus), who is essentially good. Ultimately, Marcion could not reconcile the depiction of the God who judges in the Old Testament with the Christ who redeems in the New Testament. That tension needed to be relieved for Marcion, so he chose a side and cut loose the Old Testament. Marcion was excommunicated and rejected as a heretic in AD 144, but he continued to have a strong following for several generations. Sadly, the ghost of Marcion still haunts the church today wherever we see believers put the New Testament at odds with the Old Testament, or mistakenly refer to the New Testament as grace and the Old Testament as law. There are popular Christian memes floating around the internet claiming that "wherever the Old Testament disagrees with Jesus, Jesus always wins." The impulse behind these pithy sayings appears sensible: Jesus Christ is the most complete revelation of the character, wisdom, and truth of God. But that instinct to release the tensions within Scripture prevents us from the discipleship of theological balance and the mystery of theological paradox. In other words, the "problem" isn't really a problem. Our discomfort with tension is the problem.

There is a widespread mistaken assumption that the best way to deal with tensions is to "resolve" them. It can feel like walking by a crooked picture hanging on the wall. You feel the urge to fix it, to make it "normal." But a key to engaging with Scripture is understanding that not all tensions are bad, and there is something important in the discomfort. God is far more complex than the simplicity of a book of affirmations or simple theological aphorisms and formulas. The triune God we worship is *personal*, and persons are complex. The tensions in Scripture often reflect that "thickness" of God's personality. God is immanent (nearby) and transcendent (far away). God engages us in time but exists beyond time. God judges and gives grace. God knows all people and all things, but he invites us to reveal ourselves to him (Gal. 4:9).

Sometimes we are inclined to think of tensions as bonds around us that are holding us back from a true understanding, but maybe it is better to think of Scripture's tensions more like a stringed instrument, like a guitar. Have you ever considered that a guitar makes music on the basis of tension? You pluck or strum strings of various thickness, and the sound is made based on the string snapping back and vibrating. Here the tension is not a problem to "resolve" (e.g., by cutting the string). Instead, a wise musician spends time and gains expertise learning how to tune and coordinate the tensions of the strings to make harmony. They learn how to "tune" the tensions. Part of growing as a believer is *appreciating* the benefit of the tensions in Scripture. The more we can accept this spiritual reality, the more we will receive God as he is (and not just as we would like him to be).

How to Approach Theological Problems

How do we approach reading the Bible when we have a problem with it? Or when we are facing a theological problem? Consider the following methods for navigating theological problems. First, it is critical that we embrace a *meditative* approach toward theology and biblical reading. What does it mean to meditate? To meditate is different from rigorous academic study, although the two can overlap. To study is to look at a topic or idea in a cool, objective, and heady way. This can be a good way to think about theology and biblical studies. But it can't end there. We need to come to the Bible not only as detached observers. We must also come as lovers.

An approach toward meditative reading can be found in the writings of Catholic theologian and priest Hans Urs von Balthasar. Balthasar did his academic work with rigorous intent and deep thought. But this was not his sole conviction. He also believed that the biblical text should be approached with the passion of the lover. All theology, he believed, must be done in a spirit of prayer and petition before God. He would call this "kneeling theology"—an approach of thought and reflection that, in the words of one scholar, "is often closer to prayer, to the language of devotion, to contemplation, than to the language of investigation and argument."[13]

Second, it is important that we learn to give God the benefit of the doubt. In any loving and healthy relationship that is free from abuse or toxicity, there will be moments in which the person we love says or does something that may not *seem* to be the loving thing. They may point out one of our character deficiencies or push us to be better or choose to put up boundaries. It hurts when someone who loves us does something that doesn't *feel* loving. But in those moments, we must lean on the deep belief that true love always seeks the best for the other. What might hurt us may be an act of love. In those moments, we willingly give that person the benefit of the doubt that they are acting in love. When we face a theological problem, we must cultivate an assumption of love.

Third, and last, sit on the butter. This may seem odd. But it is very important for the Christian who is seeking to love God with their whole mind. When you order pancakes at a restaurant, you will be given butter to put on top. Sometimes the butter is soft and easy to spread. But sometimes it is frozen and unmoldable. Years ago, a friend taught us what to do when you get frozen butter. Simple. You just have to sit on it for about sixty seconds. Not too long—it could melt and seep into your pants. But for a good sixty seconds, your body heat will warm it up just enough to complete that perfect pancake breakfast. What odd advice. Sit on the butter!

You might spend years wrestling with certain theological problems. This is a good thing. When we come to a hard text in the Bible, rather than run away from it, we should sit on it. That text deserves extra time, energy, and reflection. In the end, these texts in the Bible benefit us. Hard texts, it has been said, have the great benefit of softening hearts before God. The harder the theological problem and the greater our struggle with the Bible, the longer it will take to sit on it. But that's okay. Sit on it for as long as you need to. There is no rush to have an answer. In fact, you'll have everlasting time to wrestle with it.

It is easy to run away from the theological problems or difficulties in the Bible. Lord knows, ignorance is bliss. But chosen ignorance without the curiosity to learn and grow can lead, over time, to resentment, frustration, and anger. Don't run from the problems. Turn to face them. And remember that maybe that problem is the very place where God wants to do his deepest work in your soul.

Three Precious Knives

Given the cacophony of voices out there who offer a million different solutions to life's problems, it can be overwhelming to discern who to listen to, for how long, and to what effect. YouTube, TV, books, podcasts, teachers, pastors, pundits, politicians: We are constantly bombarded by advice, and we need to discern how to filter all the noise into a system of learning, thinking, and processing that will move us in the right direction of faith, hope, and love. The reality is that the "noise" isn't going to get quieter in our lives; with AirPods and smartphones with us all the time—and VR glasses in every pocket in the next decade or so—we are bound to hear more "voices" in our heads, prompting, nudging, and selling us on how to live the good life. So, we have pointed people toward a processing rubric for filtering all the noise. We call this the "three precious knives."

Imagine this: Every person or entity out there wants to impact you in some way, to sell you a product or pitch a message or promote a club to join. You want to be informed and understand what's going on in the world, but it can feel like a bombardment. What you *can* control is access. How deep are you going to let these people into your heart, mind, and soul? This is where the three precious (metaphorical) knives come in. We recommend that you think in terms of three categories of influence on you. The first and most important category is the *surgical knife*. It is wise to give the surgical knife only to the voices you want to give "all access" to your inner self, your soul, your heart. That would be people such as your close family members, your mentors, maybe your pastor, your best friend, and perhaps a few key theologians (such as C. S. Lewis and Augustine). And the Bible, of course! There is a level of trust and appreciation such that you allow these—and only these— voices to shape you in the deepest way. *Mind the surgical knife.*

Next, you have the *steak knife*. You have more of these, let's say thirty to fifty. You want to grant these voices some access to influence you—the steak knife can cut below the surface but not all the way. This would involve giving a wider group the ability to affect your thinking, but you still have caution and sensitivity not to allow their impact to go too far. This might include Christian writers in general, podcasters, and your teachers if you are a student at a Christian college or seminary. With the steak knife you have to practice discernment, sifting teachings and messages to make sure they are theologically good and right, but overall you want to allow this group to make an impact on your thought and life.

Finally, you have the *butter knife*. This is pretty much everything else you consume: TV, movies, Christian entertainment, motivational speakers, politicians, the news. It's not that these sources are necessarily *bad*, and it's not that you have to shut them out of your life. It's a matter of balance and impact. When you hand these voices the butter knife, you are listening, but they can't cut below the surface. You learn, think, discern, have fun, and enjoy, but ultimately they "spread" the information to you; they don't have access to your heart and soul.

There is freedom in the three precious knives. Once you discern who gets which knife, you can read and view and listen without fear because you have already decided how far the influence and impact can go. But we want to offer one key warning: quantity matters too. What we don't want to do is read one good theology book a year and then spend the rest of our time being influenced by comedians, pundits, and politicians. Ideally, we should be giving the majority of our learning time to Scripture, prayer, and thoughtful time with Christian mentors and friends who are going to fortify our faith and help us imitate Christ. We recommend you take some time to reflect on and perhaps even put into writing how you want to use your three precious knives. Life's not going to stop having problems, so it is worthwhile to carefully consider how we want to tackle them.

6

LET PAIN BE
THE ALTAR

Talking to God Through Our Difficulties

Emotional Displacement

Humans must have a place to take their pain. In many family systems—those complex, dynamic, and relational arrangements that profoundly shape us—we are raised with a series of unspoken expectations about where our emotions are to go. In some systems, it is normative and healthy for individuals to share with other family members about the pains and difficulties of the day. This is one of the things that marks a healthy family system. In a system that forms healthy people, space is given for the dark emotions of life to be expressed, heard, and soothed. This creates what psychologists call healthy "attachments." A relationship with healthy attachment is one in which painful emotions are expressed and blessed.

126

Some family systems do not create space for these kinds of emotions. In these systems, there are often expectations that dark, painful, or unwanted emotions are to be kept at bay, hidden, or ignored. In such environments, one is expected to hold back the pain and project joy and happiness. Why? Because someone in that family system does not have the emotional health to be able to make space for the emotional experience of another. Or the dark emotions do come out—but they come out as rageful wrath. In these family systems, pain is expressed. But it is shared in such a way that it creates more pain. In these systems, pain is either undershared or overshared. Healthy family systems make space for pain to be shared in a balanced but appropriate way.

Psychologists have long witnessed the dangers of a family system that does not make room for pain. Such is the case of Ed Kemper—a serial killer who killed seven women and one girl in the 1970s. His own tragic decisions were preceded by a tragic upbringing. After his parents' divorce, Kemper went to live with his mother in Montana. There, she proceeded to emotionally and physically abuse him. Never able to confront her lack of care, love, and affection, Kemper began to find that doing violence outside of the family provided space to mitigate his anger. Rather than being given the gift of a family where pain could be expressed, listened to, and mended, he began turning his pain outside.

A psychologist would call this "emotional displacement," an idea that goes back as far as Freud's psychoanalytic theory. Emotional displacement happens when a person cannot take the pain to the person who created it, so they take it somewhere else. Displacement is often the only way to remedy the deep pain inside. If I can't take my pain to its proper source, then I must take it to someone or something.

This psychological reality is one of the reasons that individuals who have experienced great pain at the hands of the church feel as though they have no place to go with their pain—especially not the church. We have heard the story a thousand times. When an individual goes to one of their church leaders about how they have been hurt, they are met with a leader who is unwilling—if not entirely resistant—to hear about that pain. Or the leader goes to someone in the church who has hurt that person only to find that the wrongdoer has left the church because their misdeeds have been exposed.

It requires great boldness to share about pain inflicted in the church with a leader of that church. A pastoral leader also needs great character to hear about the pain the church has caused. Sometimes pain caused within the church can't be taken to the place where it was created. This is why the internet has been therapeutic for many.

After we launched the *Slow Theology* podcast, we were pleasantly surprised at the reception to our work. People love podcasts. But we also recognize that underneath the success of our podcast, social media, and digital connection is a deep-seated and painful story. In many cases, people find in podcasts, Twitter, Instagram, Facebook, and TikTok what they cannot find in their church. People long to have a place to take their pain. But if they cannot take that pain to where it originated, they will take it somewhere else. Indeed, podcasts and social media can be examples of displacement. But in too many cases, they are necessary displacements. We *must* take our pain somewhere.

Following the murder of George Floyd, our nation saw a flood of emotion from those who were exhausted from years of bloodshed and violence toward people of color. These emotions are real—and are found throughout the Bible. They need to be listened to, and they have to go somewhere. Emotions of anger at injustice can be found in a series of psalms known as the imprecatory psalms. These are psalms of anger, rage, and outrage. Scripture is chock-full of them. Sadly, however, many of these psalms are no longer read in the lectionary or preached from the pulpit. Why? Because they are too difficult to deal with in church settings where leaders just want everyone to be clapping and gleeful and upbeat. So rather than allow rage to come into our churches, we simply don't deal with it. We become communities without anger.

The result, of course, is that many Christians who wanted to express their anger at racial injustice were not permitted to express these emotions in their churches. Their anger had to go elsewhere. One could argue that the anger we witnessed in the streets was the result of a church that made no room for anger toward injustice. The anger will go somewhere. If it is not permitted in the body of Christ, it will make its way into the streets.

We desperately need communities where we can fall apart—feeling all the pain of life. When we have a place to take our pain, our faith is given an environment where it can be cultivated in the midst of dark emotions. We will all inevitably be shaken by the pain of life. The question becomes what that pain will do for us. The pain will either propel us toward God or tempt us to abandon him. The pain of life will make us into either an Etch A Sketch or a Polaroid. In being shaken, our faith in Christ will either be shaken into oblivion—sands scattered on a gray board—or our faith will become clearer and clearer. We will all be shaken. The question is what the shaking will do to us.

Technology and the Philosophy of Now-ness

In his famous book *Future Shock*, futurist Alvin Toffler sought to explore how rapid developments in technology have shaped individuals and communities throughout history. Toffler, writing near the latter part of the twentieth century, narrates a series of firsthand accounts of individuals who were present at the Woodstock music festival, which took place August 15–18, 1969. One such teenage girl, Toffler records, described the prevailing spirit of the event she had personally experienced. Everything about Woodstock revolved around experiencing the present moment. Literally isolated from the outside world on a dairy farm in upstate New York, participants were invited to cast aside their commitments and outside lives to embrace living exclusively in the present. "We're more oriented to the present," the teenage woman says. "It's like doing what you want to do now. . . . If you stay anywhere very long you get into a planning thing. . . . So you just move on."[1]

When Toffler penned his book, he aptly called this the spirit of the age—what he dubbed the "philosophy of 'now-ness.'"[2] That was in 1970. What was an emerging spirit of the age in the 1960s was surely only in its infancy stage and pointed to what was to come. Since the countercultural age of the 1960s, "presentism" is now in full harvest. As human societies—especially in the West—have been moved along by a seemingly endless parade of rapid technological advancements, the human experience has been entirely reframed. Letting go of the past and ignoring the future has become the epitome of much of our age. Everything is about the present. There is no future or waiting for the future. Other thinkers have connected this very spirit with what we see transpiring in human sexuality. Because there is no future and no judgment, do what you wish now, so long as nobody is hurt.[3]

The spirit of now-ness cuts off the present from the future and the past. In the first few chapters of Genesis, we are introduced to a serpent who enters the garden of Eden. He approaches the woman and offers a promise. If she were to eat from the forbidden tree, "You will not certainly die. . . . Your eyes will be opened, and you will be like God, knowing good and evil" (Gen. 3:4–5). Underneath this temptation to eat from the forbidden tree is the temptation of now-ness. "You will not certainly die," in part, is the alluring thought that there will be no judgment, no future reckoning, nothing that will hold them accountable. Interestingly, the first doctrine that the devil denies is the doctrine of judgment. Which is brilliant—because if he can cut us off from believing we will be held to account, he can get us to do anything.

Life since Eden has increasingly become a world that sees itself as being liberated from the distant past and the future. Everything is about today. Social statements such as YOLO ("You Only Live Once") encourage us to cast off any notion of living in light of some future judgment or reckoning. Toffler cleverly calls this spirit the vision of "social planlessness."[4] Don't think about or anticipate the future. Live in the now. Technology presents a dangerous deception: It dislocates us from the future and the past and idolizes all things present.

The clever human use of technology can be so treacherous and dangerous. People often turn to technology as a means of escaping pain. It can distract us easily—at a moment's notice, we can dive into binge-watching a show to forget the stressors of the day. Technology can allow us to become spectators of our pain rather than help us process it in a healthy way. We may find ourselves doomscrolling late at night, channeling our anger toward problems in the world instead of confronting it in our own lives. Technology can also become a means of avoiding relationships. An addiction to video games can become a way to avoid conversations or to sidestep forging important emotional connections. Technology is often the thing we use to reject the pain of the present.

When the purpose of life is constricted merely to the present, to the immediate, there is a diminished capacity to hold pain. Because the present holds the weight of everything, we are tempted to export dark emotions to another time. If now is everything, then now must be guarded against an attack of pain. Or we take the pain of the present and make it everything.

A few chapters after humans are banished from Eden, the human community endures a flood. Their wickedness had become so great that God could no longer stand by and watch. Choosing a family through whom he would restore the earth, God brings Noah and his family through the flood to begin a new chapter. On the ark, God makes a promise: He would never again destroy the earth by flood. In the chapters that follow, humans repopulate the earth and eventually settle on the plains of Babel. There they build a tower reaching into the sky. This technological monolith is a place of false worship, but in the context of God's promise, it also symbolizes a lack of trust. Instead of relying on God's assurance that no flood would destroy them, they use technology to protect themselves from the pain and fear of devastation.

Sometimes one of the hardest things to do is to detach ourselves from the devices we use to escape and instead sit down and cry. Rather than using technology as a means of escaping the flood of tears that life in this world brings, we can embrace the deep, dark, and painful emotions. Better yet, we can bring them to God, who weeps with us. Technology can become an escape from pain. But true Christian spirituality always invites us to go to the pain rather than run away from it.

The False Promises of the Internet

The internet offers us two core false promises, each of which subverts our spiritual formation into Christ. First, the rise of the internet has created an environment where one can project a false self into the world. This is particularly the case with social media. Take the stories of Yvette Vickers and Madison Holleran. Yvette Vickers was an eighty-three-year-old former Playboy playmate. After her neighbors noticed that she had not come out of her house for six months, and that her mail was accumulating, they decided to investigate. Entering her home, they found the mummified body of the woman. She'd been dead for some time.

Inside, they discovered something odd. One of the neighbors—exploring Vickers's phone records—discovered that she had not been in contact with any of her family and friends. She had, however, been in near constant contact with her fans from around the globe. As Stephen Marche, the investigative reporter who wrote on the story, described, "Vickers's web of connections had grown broader but shallower, as has happened to most of us."[5]

A similar story is found in Madison Holleran. Young and seemingly full of life and hope, Holleran was nineteen years old with the world before her. From the looks of it, she had everything going for her. She was a successful athlete at the University of Pennsylvania. She enjoyed the rich relationships of a good family and friends. All seemed well. In January 2014, however, she placed a photo of herself as a child, some Godiva chocolates for her dad and some jewelry for her mom, and some cookies for the grandparents on the ledge of a nine-story parking garage and jumped. Holleran's death shocked everyone, including those who knew her on social media. In the months leading up to her death, Holleran's life looked happy, fruitful, and hopeful. One journalist wrote that Madison's Instagram feed "was filled with shots that seemed to confirm everyone's expectations."[6]

Both tragic tales crack open the door just enough for us to see how we can be deceived by what the internet provides. It is increasingly possible for us to be known for the image we want to be known for—and go unseen for who we really are. In the one story, someone seeks connection with those they will never know in person, all the while cutting off the nurturing ties of friends and family. The other story tells of someone who *appeared* to be well but secretly was filled with sadness and despair. The internet offers us the false promise that we can curate an image of someone lovable. The problem, of course, is that people end up loving the image we have created rather than loving us for who we really are.

The second false promise of the internet is that of immediacy. Immediacy can be a blessing. For example, when a Christian encounters a theological problem that vexes them, they can do a quick search to see who has helpful information to resolve this issue. Podcasts have largely filled this need. At a moment's notice, we can find an almost endless array of curated content that helps navigate the challenges we're facing. One can now log into ChatGPT, ask a series of deep theological questions, and receive in seconds a well-written, articulated answer to one's quandary.

But this immediacy also leads to another set of problems. We may have the answer we are looking for, but that doesn't mean we truly understand it. Nor did we have to do anything to acquire it. This is one of the most pressing dangers of accessing immediate knowledge: It gives us the answers without cultivating in us patience, long-suffering, and forbearance. As theologian Peter Williams writes, "Fast information is to the brain like fast food is to the body. Good food takes time to prepare. So does good information."[7] Finding the right answers is not always the goal of theology. What really matters is the process of becoming Christlike on the journey.

We are deceived into wanting what is efficient and fast in the spiritual life. When we look at how Scripture talks about this life, we find that it is often through the use of agrarian metaphors. The spiritual life isn't built or produced through a mechanical efficiency. Paul, in describing the church in Corinth, says that he had planted the seed of the gospel, Apollos had watered it, but God was the one who made it grow (1 Cor. 3:5–9). Life with God is like a slowly developing garden in which many people contribute—but only God makes it grow.

Slow to Speak in Prayer

The alternative to these technological dangers is the life of prayer. James, the brother of Jesus, seeks to outline the normative conversational ethic for the follower of Christ: "My dear brothers and sisters, take note of this: Everyone should be quick to listen, slow to speak and slow to become angry, because human anger does not produce the righteousness that God desires" (James 1:19–20). The community formed around the worship of Christ should not be one where people are talking over one another to get in their ideas, it should not be a space where people are given quickly to rage and dissension, and it must, above all, be a place where listening and honoring are exalted and normative virtues. James wants us to see Christian community through this lens.

We are elsewhere commanded to have a similar approach to the way we listen and relate to God. In Ecclesiastes, for example, God's people are commanded:

> Do not be quick with your mouth,
>   do not be hasty in your heart
>   to utter anything before God.
> God is in heaven
>   and you are on earth,
>   so let your words be few. (5:2)

The wise preacher of Ecclesiastes sees a problem in coming to God with too many words. It is as though people have come to God in order to instruct him. Or they are coming to offer vows to get God off their back. Sometimes they are hasty in what they say to him. Not only are we commanded to bring as few words as possible to God—just as Jesus warned against the practices of the pagans who "keep on babbling" to try and get God's attention (Matt. 6:7). We are also commanded to be careful not to make rash or unthoughtful promises to God.

This stands in contrast to much of the teaching we often hear on Christian prayer. The more we talk to God, we are told, the more we will receive. But the danger in such an ethic of prayer is that we begin to see God as a divine Santa whose sole purpose is to give us what we've wished for—and that we have leverage over him because we've been good little boys and girls. What a dangerous view of prayer, indeed! Just as we are invited to be slow to speak in our relationships with people, we are invited by the same biblical text to be slow to speak to God. This does not mean we do not speak. It just means we come to God with wisdom and reflection on what it is we are actually asking for.

Prayer should be marked more by presence than requests. When the sole purpose of one's prayer life becomes minimized to requests for things, it begins to lose its power and vitality.

Learning How to Lament (or, How to Fight Well with God)

John Gottman and his wife, Julie Schwartz Gottman, are both psychologists who have dedicated their careers to strengthening relationships. They have written, separately and together, a number of bestsellers, including *The Seven Principles for Making Marriage Work, Eight Dates: Essential Conversations for a Lifetime of Love,* and *The Man's Guide to Women: Scientifically Proven Secrets from the Love Lab About What Women Really Want.* They have distinguished themselves as world-leading experts on marriage.

Their latest work, *Fight Right,* focuses on how couples fight and how they can recover from conflict well.[8] The Gottmans have long argued that most Americans believe a popular myth that fighting and conflict are inherently problematic and that "good couples" never fight. There is no evidence to back up that assumption. How much a couple fights does not correspond directly with the overall happiness of the marriage. A couple could rate relatively high on the happiness index and still have conflict regularly. Inversely, a couple could fight very infrequently and yet have a very unhealthy and unhappy relationship. The bottom line is that *frequency* of conflict doesn't indicate something bad in a relationship; rather, the key is *how* you fight and, more importantly, your willingness to seek repair. The Gottmans encourage paying attention to the ratio of positive to negative interactions. Having negative interactions, even numerous negative interactions, is not a relationship deal-breaker, they explain. But for a relationship to succeed and thrive, the positive interactions must be much higher in frequency than the negative ones. (The magic ratio is five to one; on average, happy and thriving couples have five times the number of positive interactions as negative ones.)

The Gottmans are psychologists, not theologians, and their advice is geared toward marriage relationships, but their insights have some clear applications for how we relate to a relational God who made us for a deep and intimate relationship with him. And the Bible seems to back up the Gottmans' claim that fighting itself is not a problem. In any kind of close relationship (whether with a spouse, a parent, a child, or a close friend), there are bound to be times of disagreement, hurt feelings, or just plain grumpiness. In the Bible we find that God's people had just this kind of close relationship with their covenant God; they enjoyed extraordinary moments of intimacy and connection, while at other moments conflict and anger were present.

For example, when Job is suffering from so many hurts and losses in his life despite his innocence and righteousness, he complains to Yahweh:

> I loathe my very life;
>> therefore I will give free rein to my complaint
>> and speak out in the bitterness of my soul.
> I say to God: Do not declare me guilty,
>> but tell me what charges you have against me.
> Does it please you to oppress me,
>> to spurn the work of your hands,
>> while you smile on the plans of the wicked? (Job 10:1–3)

Strong words, but this reflects both the close relationship that Job felt he had with Yahweh and what he perceived as the sting of betrayal. Job felt justified in complaining to Yahweh because he valued this special relationship he had with his God. Job models what the Christian tradition has called "lament," or reverential complaints directed at God. We'll return to that in a moment.

The Gottmans, again, affirm that two people having conflict in a relationship is not a bad thing. It's normal—so normal, in fact, that it is expected. When two people are trying to live one life together, they are bound to offend or hurt each other. Again, the frequency of fighting *by itself* is not the sign of a bad relationship or a high risk of divorce. However, they have identified a handful of indicators that do suggest extreme unhealthiness in a relationship. They call these the "Four Horsemen of the Apocalypse":

Criticism: Attacking the person (rather than the specific issues).

Contempt: Mean-spirited statements and behavior, like name-calling, mockery, and sarcasm. These are petty tools calculated to make someone feel like a loser.

Defensiveness: The accused takes a posture of complete innocence and cannot accept criticism, sometimes even turning the tables and blaming the other person.

Stonewalling: The listener responds to a verbal attack or complaint by turning away and avoiding their partner. It is often a last resort when other response attempts have seemed to fail.

Regarding the fourth horseman (stonewalling), the Gottmans have said that when couples turn away from each other and stop communicating, this almost certainly spells disaster for the relationship, and divorce is all but inevitable. One can see how much of this applies to our relationship with God. The Bible reminds us that having complaints against God is normal, it is expected, and there is a long and rich tradition of biblical lament that teaches us how to bring our frustrations to God. But the Gottmans are really on to something when they warn against stonewalling, and certainly we try to stonewall God as a defense mechanism. To be brutally honest, when we build that wall tall enough, strong enough, and thick enough, we in effect sever the relationship.

Now, you might have grown up in a family system that practiced avoidance, where you prevent conflict at all costs through making jokes about problems, walking on eggshells, or just keeping physical distance when things are awkward or heated. Those habits can carry over and affect our relationship with God. But it's important to heed the warnings of people such as the Gottmans. Blocking someone out of your life—even and *especially* God—is inevitably a relationship killer. While the alternative is "fighting it out," at least there is hope for learning how to fight *well* with God. In a moment, we are going to offer some advice, but we encourage you first to familiarize yourself with key lament texts in the Bible.

Biblical Lament

Scripture offers us a treasure trove of songs intended to help us wrestle through the pain of life. One of these sections is from the Psalms. There are various types of psalms, including a category known as lament psalms. These are songs used by individuals or groups to, in the words of scholars, "express struggles, suffering, or disappointment to the Lord."[9] Surprisingly, a large number of psalms fall into this category—more than any other type. In fact, about 40 percent of all the psalms are considered laments. These psalms of protest, giving voice to the anger and sadness over the way things are, serve as a tool to help God's people process their emotions.

These psalms invite us to many things:

Be honest and transparent. As we bring our hurts and anger to God, we are encouraged to be open and honest. As you read biblical lament texts, you will notice that holy leaders such as Moses or David or Jeremiah are sometimes heated and forthright. They don't hold back their thoughts and feelings.

Name God's character. One of the reasons why God's people in Scripture complain to him is because they have high expectations based on what they know about God's character and promises. We encourage you to verbally name back to God what he has affirmed about himself in the Word: God's righteousness, his holiness, his love, his commitment to justice, his promises to make things right.

Invite God to act. Typically, biblical lament petitions God to change the situation, to behave in light of his revealed character, to act in faithfulness and love. Invite God to move in power to make things right.

Affirm God's faithfulness and commit to hope. This is the most difficult aspect of lament because it requires having faith that God will indeed make things right, somehow, in the end. It acknowledges, as Paul explains, that we see now, in this world, only part of the whole of God's reality, like trying to see something through a mirror reflection in dim lighting (1 Cor. 13:12). One day we will have a better chance to see things from God's perspective, but our duty now is to lean into faith and hope.

The Gospels of Matthew and Mark both record the saying on the lips of Jesus from the cross: "My God, my God, why have you forsaken me?" (Mark 15:34; Matt. 27:46). Jesus was in anguish, plunged into darkness, and he cried his eyes and his heart out. Jesus was quoting the first line of Psalm 22, a psalm of David and hymn of lament. It begins with a series of questions, wondering why God has disappeared in the hour in which he was needed most. David lists all the ways that he is trapped in a position of danger, shame, and hopelessness. Then he desperately calls for rescue and redemption. "Deliver me from the sword. . . . Rescue me from the mouth of the lions; save me from the horns of the wild oxen" (vv. 20–21). David intermixes praise and blessing on God throughout the psalm, acknowledging God's loyalty and goodness. David also imagines a time when all will be made well and all will recognize the praiseworthiness of Yahweh. All nations will turn to him, David foresees: "They will proclaim his righteousness, declaring to a people yet unborn: He has done it!" (v. 31). When Jesus hung on a cross and uttered the opening words of this psalm, he surely knew the entirety of David's lament and he would have been reared to lament faithfully as David his ancestor modeled it. While Jesus uttered out loud only the opening words—"Why have you forsaken me?"—as a devout Jewish man, Jesus was initiating the healing practice of lament. Jesus did not die on the cross wondering whether the Father was good or evil or whether he was trustworthy or unreliable. Jesus's "cry of derelection" (as it is called) represents his identification with the plight of humanity, his sense of resonance with the haunting questions that King David was asking almost a thousand years before Golgotha.

It is a spiritual paradox, but Jesus's identification with the feeling of being forsaken by God is actually a gift to us now. Jesus paved the way for us who believe, even when we feel deep anguish and exasperation and cannot reconcile God's promises with our present experiences. Jesus reminds us that it is actually okay to fight with God, as long as we fight well.

As the Gottmans have helpfully shown, the worst thing in a relationship is not the fighting. There's good fighting and there's bad fighting, and the goal is to learn how to fight fairly and fight well (with God and with each other). But the real spiritual danger is when we stonewall God and take our hearts and souls somewhere else. There is always hope for healing (what the Gottmans call "repair") as long as there is gracious communication. But when the communication stops, when we put up walls against God, when we try to will God's nonexistence, then the death of the relationship is all but certain. There is a wise saying that gets passed around: "To cry is human. But to lament is Christian."[10] Lament is the biblical practice that we have been given to process our hurt and anger *with* God and not just *against* God. Lament actually *invites* us to be openly upset with God, not to push him away but to invite him to respond. Not long after Jesus questioned the presence of God, he was raised from death to life. Lament, in the end, is hope-filled desperation.

The Bible is a mishmash of different kinds of writings. These different literary styles are called "genres." And there are many: historical narrative, fictional stories called "parables," poetry, and so on. Each of these genres carries with it a unique meaning and purpose—and is to be read in a unique way. The historical accounts of the resurrection necessitate a different kind of reading than the parables. Not all of the Bible is to be read literally in the sense that every part of the Bible is to be read as historical fact. When the prophet Isaiah tells us that God is like a mother hen, he is not telling us that the Creator of the universe has feathers. Rather, he is insisting that the God of the universe cares for everything he has made in the same way a mother cares for her children. Yet when Matthew, Mark, Luke, and John insist that Jesus rose from the grave, they want us to arrive at a place of faith, where we can rest our knowledge on the historical event of the empty tomb.

The medium, as Marshall McLuhan famously wrote, is the message.[11] That is, we are shaped by more than just what is being said. We are also shaped by the medium through which it is stated. This is important when we read one particular genre in the biblical story: poetry. Scholars estimate that approximately one-third of the biblical story is written in poetic form. In fact, we have an entire section of the Old Testament devoted to this kind of writing—a collection of writings that comprises books such as the Psalms, Proverbs, Ecclesiastes, and many others. For the ancient biblical author, there were some things about God that could be expressed only through the particular medium of poetry.

One of these books is Job. Job is an ancient tale of a man who loses it all. Everything—his family, his occupation, his land, his health—has been taken from him through a series of storms. Job seeks to narrate one of the most painful human experiences one can come to know: suffering. One of the unique features of Job is its vocabulary. Job uses more Hebrew words that are used only once in the Bible than any other Old Testament book. The vocabulary is a dizzying array of exotic and difficult words that are, at times, nearly impossible to translate. Another feature of Job is that the brunt of the book, on the theme of suffering, is written in poetry. Almost all of Job, after the first two chapters, uses long-standing poetry that gives language to Job's horrific experience.

These two literary features are exceptionally instructive for people who are walking through the experience of suffering. When one suffers, it often feels as though what you are going through is something no one else has experienced. The depth of pain almost feels as if you have been plucked from the normalcy of life. That Job utilizes such an exotic vocabulary speaks to this experience. The normal language that people who are not suffering use to describe the experience of suffering rarely, if ever, connects. This difficult vocabulary, no doubt, connects to the reality of human life—no language can fully explain what it is like to go through an experience like Job's.

But more than this, the Bible's description of loss and suffering are narrated in a form of literature that inherently necessitates slowing down. As Eugene Peterson wisely writes, "Poetry cannot be hurried. We must slow our minds (and in prayer, our lives) to the pace of the poet's breathing, phrases separated by pauses. . . . Poetry requires equal time to be given to sounds and silences."[12] The very medium of the sacred writing about suffering requires the reader to go particularly slowly and methodically through the text—entering into the exotic words and poetic structure with the intent of reflecting and spending time in deep thought.

Clearly, for the Bible, suffering is never something we can simply rush through. Slowing down and allowing it to shape you is often what brings the glory that God desires it to have. By embracing a posture toward pain like the one modeled by Scripture, we give ourselves the necessary space in our walk with Christ to be able to process the difficulties of life.

BELIEVE TOGETHER

One Faith, One Body, and Communal Theology

A Faith That Is Shared

Dwight Peterson was a gifted biblical scholar and celebrated teacher known for his quick wit and biting sense of humor. Peterson had been a paraplegic since he was eighteen years old. Despite enduring decades of struggle and difficulty, this didn't stop him from having an accomplished career over the span of fifteen years in which he served his students as professor at Eastern University (Pennsylvania). However, a major infection sent Dwight to hospice care in his home, where he would eventually pass. During his illness, Dwight gave an interview offering unfettered access into his personal life. He was struggling with his faith in Christ.[1] He admitted to his audience that there had been desperate and despairing times when he felt as though his faith had virtually left him. But he also admitted to finding hope: by relying on a short story from the Gospels in Mark 2:1–5.

The text may be familiar: Jesus has arrived in Capernaum, where he is staying at someone's home. Predictably, the crowds swell to massive numbers in hopes of a chance to see and hear the upstart revolutionary teacher, healer, and exorcist. Four men are recorded as bringing a paralytic man to Jesus. But when they arrive, they cannot find a way into the house. So they resort to climbing onto the roof, digging a hole in it, and lowering the man down to Jesus. Mark records that when Jesus observes the faith of these friends of the man, he says to the paralytic, "Son, your sins are forgiven" (v. 5). Dwight confesses to having heard this story countless times growing up. As a New Testament scholar, he'd studied and taught the Gospel of Mark numerous times. But this story had never made much sense to him—that is, until he sat in the loneliness and isolation and darkness of hospice care. Desperate to hear from God and struggling to make sense of God's presence and goodness, the story came to life.

Dwight's understanding of Mark's short healing narrative became illuminated on one occasion when he was visited by a close friend. Dwight admitted to him, "I can't find my faith." Dwight braced himself for looks of disappointment or judgment. But this was not what he received. The friend simply said back, "It's okay, we have it for you." Almost immediately, Mark 2 began to take on a profoundly new meaning for Dwight in hospice. On many occasions, we are told, Jesus would heal someone as a result of *their* personal faith in him. But something different seemed to be going on here. In the story of the paralytic (Dwight preferred to call him "the cripple," feeling a special bond with the man's situation), Jesus brings about the healing as he sees the faith of his *friends*. As he is interviewed, Dwight rightly recognizes that it is necessary for every person to place their faith in Jesus. But this story was a salutary reminder that the church is a community of faith. Believers support one another just like the paralytic's friends were determined to get him to Jesus no matter what. Dwight called this a "wild grace," the gift of having others carry your faith when your own faith is fading or failing. Dwight's journey through hospice care would continue for an additional three years before he passed away. Still, in those last years, the celebrated teacher found great hope and assurance that his faith was not standing alone. He held hands with a whole community that was believing alongside him.

Thinking about faith this way may be an awkward fit—especially for those living in the Western context. Environments that have been shaped by the Enlightenment can see relying on and sharing the faith of another as the ultimate sin. From birth, we are overtly instructed to "think for ourselves" and "question everything" and "to thine own self be true." Pithy little statements like these are not-so-subtle indictments from an individualist culture that does not value the vitality and need for communal, shared belief. But this obsession with individualized faith is a relatively new idea going back to the thinking of seventeenth-century philosopher René Descartes. Entering a cave of quiet seclusion and seeking to uncover what the truth was, the philosopher emerged with a famous saying: *Cogito, ergo sum.* "I think, therefore I am."

Little has shaped Western culture more than this sentiment. For our purposes, it is critical to notice the sheer *individuality* of Descartes's statement. Descartes believed that knowledge and truth can be known through what *I* can know from *myself*. Cultures that follow this tradition tend to make the individual the center of the universe.[2] As James K. A. Smith comically reflects,

> Racked with anxiety because his prior certainties have become shipwrecked on the shores of later doubt, Descartes finds himself in an existential crisis: if things that have seemed so certain to him can later be unveiled as false, then how can he be certain about anything? Trying to tackle this angst head-on, Descartes retreats to isolation in a room for several days simply to think his way through the problem. How different would the world be if Descartes could have just gotten a date.[3]

No doubt, thinking and believing on an individual level has profound merit and necessity. We each must place our faith in

Christ individually. Still, individual faith has its exceptional liabilities. By believing all alone, we greatly increase the possibility of overlooking and ignoring voices that can hold us to account. It is the individualist belief structure of the West that has conveniently overlooked and ignored those voices that may draw us back to the heart of Jesus. Theology must be a communal act. Understanding the communal nature of faith—how we need to believe and come to rely on the faith of others—reshapes the way we think about and process who God is. The salvation that we experience in Christ cannot be monopolized by any of us.

Scripture affirms this. The apostle Paul gives us an extraordinary glimpse into this notion of a faith *community* in his famous body metaphor first articulated in 1 Corinthians 12. The Corinthian church was a textbook case study in immature faith. Instead of being a gracious and united community, groups were split off and at war with one another, each one trying to prove themselves superior and more "spiritual" than the other. Paul sternly warns them that only at their own peril do they fail to understand that they are all one body composed of many different parts, and *all* of the parts are necessary for a healthy body to function well. Their differences benefit the whole. The parts cannot actually function on their own. The eye is important, but not if it is separate from the rest of the body. The body would be destroyed if the parts turned against one another. And there is every good reason to support and care for one another: "If one part suffers, every part suffers with it; if one part is honored, every part rejoices with it" (12:26). Paul is pointing to a kind of ecosystem of faith. While each person must be individually converted and die and rise with Christ in baptism, we live out our faith together as one spiritual body. When one part is hurting, the other parts must jump into action, strengthening it. Because all parts contribute meaningfully to the whole, no part should struggle on its own. The upshot is this: We were not made to live out our life of faith in Jesus Christ by ourselves. Paul reinforces this point in his letter to the Ephesians. Just as all believers share one Lord, they also share in one baptism and one faith (Eph. 4:5–6). We're saved by faith alone, but we're not meant to live out our faith alone!

When Jude reflects on the "salvation we share" (v. 3),[4] he is giving a whole new paradigm for the Christian story than the one we may be used to or even comfortable with. We may follow Christ through faith. But we live out that faith *together*, interconnected, interrelated, and in constant need of communal experience. Doing the work of theology together is harder, slower, and more difficult. But the end result is bound to be clearer and truer.

Paul's "body" metaphor and Jude's communal salvation language are profoundly insightful in terms of understanding how we care for and support one another. All of nature, it turns out, is deeply communal. In recent years, forest ecologists have been studying how trees are connected (at the root level, underground) in a forest. These scientists point to certain mycorrhizal fungi that grow on tree roots and form "networks" that connect trees throughout an ecosystem. Through these fungi networks, trees "communicate" with one another and even share water, carbon, nitrogen, and other nutrients. Because trees (like all living organisms) are inclined toward their own survival, they respond when they become aware that a fellow tree is hurt or dying. Respected ecologist Suzanne Simard recounts a case study where a Douglas fir, which was injured by insects, sent warnings to a nearby ponderosa pine, which led the pine to create a defensive mechanism to protect itself from the pests. Simard also explains how healthy trees have been known to share water for mutual survival.[5]

Just as trees need one another, so do we. Especially in how we think about God.

Communal Correction

Theology is best done together. This is not only because it shapes us as people—and strengthens the relationships of the church—but also because doing theology together helps sharpen and correct our thinking. In academia, when an expert in a field writes an academic journal article, it is a much different process than when someone posts a blog or a tweet. Because of the novelty of instantaneous technological communication, we can publish to the world in nearly seconds. In academic writing, the process of putting one's ideas out there can take months if not years. When finished, the article is submitted and sent to blind reviewers, who weigh its merit; if accepted, the article is reworked, resubmitted, sent out for peer review, and then published. The whole journey requires a community of scholars who help sharpen the author's ideas.

For many Christians, it may feel a tad uncomfortable to learn that much of the preaching and teaching in the church today goes through little if any communal scrutiny before it is taught. Not that it would be possible for pastors—who are already overburdened—to be able to develop such a system. But much of what we learn from the pulpit on Sundays comes from a man or woman who has spent their week isolated, in an office, preparing what they are going to say. This can be good and it can be bad. It can be good if the person is wise and trained and knows the needed nuance and balance for good theology. It is bad when the person lacks these skills.

Through its history, however, the church offers us countless beautiful stories of how it can be corrected in community. Consider, for instance, the story of Catherine of Siena (1347–80). Catherine was the twenty-fourth of her parents' twenty-five children. When she was a child, she had a dreamlike vision about Jesus that altered the entirety of her life. The fourteenth century was not an easy time for a woman to be able to lead in the church. Ministry for a woman at the time was almost exclusively relegated to being a cloistered nun. But she knew God had a different role for her. During the Black Plague—a pandemic that would take the lives of millions of people—she gave her life and energy to serve people as they were dying.

But her ministry went even further than this. At the time, the papacy had been relocated from Rome to Avignon, France. In what has been called the "Babylonian captivity of the church," the church was rife with excessive wealth, power grabs, and moral depravity. Catherine saw this and took action. One of her letters to Pope Gregory XI has survived, and it is confronting and clear. She writes,

> Most holy father, your poor unworthy daughter Catherine, servant and slave of the servants of Jesus Christ, writes to you in his precious blood, with desire to see you a good shepherd. I tell you in the name of Christ crucified, you must use the instrument of severity. With the hand of love and the rod of justice, let not human respect hinder you. The wolf is carrying away your sheep, and there is no one to deliver them.[6]

Confronting what she saw as the spiritual decay of the people of God, Catherine's words had a deep effect. The pope, reading the words of this tenacious and holy woman, was moved to the heart. By 1377, Gregory XI returned the papacy to Rome and instigated reforms. All because of the persistent passion of a woman who knew God had called her to something important.

Theological correction—like the kind we see in the life of Catherine—is possible only in the context of community. Too often, to protect ourselves from encountering such corrective words and needing to act as a result, we opt to go it alone. Sadly, as we all have seen, those who are most convinced that their theology is airtight and accurate can tend to be the most inflexible and cold-shouldered people one could meet.

But this does not need to be the only way forward. Scripture is replete with monumental moments in which theological community leads to theological correction—and fruit that comes as a result. In Acts 18, a man named Apollos, who had been teaching "about Jesus accurately" (v. 25), had taken on an incomplete and inaccurate view of baptism—only knowing the baptism of John. Soon, an early church power team of Priscilla and Aquila came to him to confront the issue. They opened their home, created a space of hospitality, and then "explained to him the way of God more adequately" (v. 26). Soon, Apollos would leave—having been corrected by this married couple—and go to Achaia, where we are told he was a "great help to those who by grace had believed" (v. 27). His ministry is said to have continued with great power and authority.

The correction that took the ministry of Apollos to a higher level was possible only because he opened himself up to it. Without his willingness to do so, he would have likely continued to teach, but he would have missed out on rising to the level of the dynamic ministry that was a direct result of receiving instruction from his community.

Together Theology

The church is designed by God to serve as the ideal space for God's people to reflect on him. "Theology," Karl Barth famously wrote, "is a function of the church."[7] Theology is meant for the church. It's essential, therefore, to ask, What is the church? Throughout the writings of the New Testament, the word "church" is represented by the word *ekklēsia*. Its use remains rather surprising given how sparingly it is used. The word is rarely used in the Gospels of Matthew, Mark, Luke, and John.[8] Moreover, the word is not distinctively Christian. In Greco-Roman culture, an *ekklēsia* was a description of a legal gathering of people within an urban context who were gathering to discuss the welfare of a city.[9]

When this word was adopted by the earliest Christians, it took on a whole new meaning. *Ekklēsia* became that community where people came together to share a love and worship of King Jesus. The church, then, is that vibrant community of people from diverse times, places, and cultures, united in their pursuit of worshiping

Christ together. Despite being sparingly mentioned in the Gospels, the *ekklēsia* becomes the centerpiece of conversation by the time we come to the book of Acts, the Epistles, and the book of Revelation. What began as a group of twelve ragtag disciples became a movement that was growing throughout the Roman Empire. Given that the Epistles, in most cases, were written before the Gospels, there's good evidence that Paul had a hand in popularizing the use of the word *ekklēsia* to describe this multiethnic, cross-cultural community of people who lived under allegiance to Jesus Christ.

What does this have to do with theology? In Paul's writings to the churches, there is a noticeable tension: Paul always balanced both the individual and communal nature of these local expressions. Paul was writing to actual gatherings and communities of people on the ground. None of these letters are the same—each tackles a different set of issues and concerns. On the one hand, Paul speaks into the individual realities of these churches, knowing they had their own personality. Yet, on the other hand, Paul advocates for a universal set of teachings that remains the same between churches. In 1 Corinthians 4:17 Paul makes reference to that "which agrees with what I teach everywhere in every church." Later, in the same letter, he references the teachings that he "lay[s] down in all the churches" (7:17).

These two polarities—of the universal and distinct personality of each church—reframe our understanding of the nature of the church in a profound way. Every church was different. It had its own flavor, personality, and set of problems. But these distinct expressions made up a church that was part of something bigger than itself. The words of Jesus to the seven churches in Revelation 1–3 reveal that the Spirit speaks different things to different churches. Why? Because each one is different. Yet despite this individuality, there are teachings to be handed down that Paul believed should be the same everywhere. Similarly, today, it is not only the reality—but it is also good—that each individual local church has its own taste, touch, and smell. The church *should* be diverse. Yet it is equally important that the church—in its differences—recognize that it is the same Spirit who brings them together around the same communal truths. This is a great mystery. Paul speaks of the Holy Spirit as the one who both unifies the church and gives different gifts to each person. The church is a "reconciled diversity."[10]

Being a community under the King is a beautiful reality—one that should take decades to truly appreciate. But it is crucial that we be equally honest: It also creates more friction. Making decisions together is always more challenging than making decisions alone. When we make decisions alone, we don't have to think about or even consider what another person may have to say on a given topic. We can go here and there as the sole deciders in our life. And while this may seem liberating and life-giving, in the end, we miss out on something significant when we go it alone. Making decisions alone can speed up the process. But making decisions together can provide wisdom that can bring more fruitfulness than we ever could have imagined. By doing theology alone, we arrive at conclusions faster. But doing theology alone was never God's intent. And it increases the chance that we may distort the church's message that has been handed down for generations.

Consider a marriage. In any covenantal relationship of fidelity, there will be times when decisions need to be made about some move, a career change, or how to best raise a child. These sorts of forks in the road affect more than just one person. They affect the two people in the marriage. They can also affect the children of that married couple—to say nothing of the community, church, and employers in which they are already in relationship with. A decision impacts many. In a marriage, if only one person's perspective and thought is considered, it can lead not only to resentment and anger but also to decisions that end up hurting all the parties involved. As a general rule, in Christian marriage, it is wise for both people to listen to each other and make a decision together. Otherwise, one person ends up running ahead without the other person feeling involved.

Communal decisions are an important part of more than just a healthy marriage—they were clearly an important part of the early church. As the early Christian community began to expand through the Roman Empire, a major issue presented itself: Should Gentiles who had come to believe in Jesus be allowed to follow Jesus without having to undergo a conversion to Jewish culture with its kosher laws and circumcision? The issue was pressing and would have reverberations for generations to come. What did the early church opt to do? We are told simply that "the apostles and elders met to consider this question" (Acts 15:6).

For a season of discernment, prayer, and listening, the early power brokers in the church gathered together in Jerusalem to discuss how the church would handle this theological question. The decision about how to handle the Gentiles was not put on one person's shoulders. The early church did not operate—at least in the context of the book of Acts—according to Moses's style of leadership, where one person came off the mountain to tell everyone what was going to happen. They operated in a communal context to wrestle with these theological issues together. Their decision took time, energy, and great debate, even bringing Paul and Barnabas into "sharp dispute" (15:2) with the apostles in the city.

The decision those early leaders made, that circumcision was not a requirement, was one of the most consequential in early church history. They simply write,

> It seemed good to the Holy Spirit and to us not to burden you with anything beyond the following requirements: You are to abstain from food sacrificed to idols, from blood, from the meat of strangled animals and from sexual immorality. You will do well to avoid these things. (15:28–29)

Because of that consensus, the early church was able to move forward without requiring Gentiles to undergo a cultural conversion to follow Jesus. This choice to make a theological decision *together* would impact the world for thousands of years. It may have slowed the church down, but the church also became stronger.

There are many instances in the history of the church when theology was done communally—gathering the wisdom of the whole church and the whole counsel of God. When this has not been prioritized, the consequences have been quite serious. The Great Schism between the Western and Eastern church in the eleventh century was due, in large part, to the fact that the Western church had changed the Nicene Creed without consulting the Eastern church. While there have been many strides toward reconciliation between both communities, the fracture has lasted nearly a thousand years—all because the church did not do its theological work together.

For many pastors, this principle of the need for communal theology can be the difference between faithfulness and the abandonment of faith. For instance, when we begin to make theological decisions about what is good and true based on engagement with a few videos on TikTok or a compelling set of YouTube videos, we are making theological decisions apart from the community we have been walking with. This is just one illustration of how we often make theological decisions everywhere *but* among the people who are following Jesus together in a local church.

Or when we desire to wrestle with a sensitive theological topic (such as sexuality and gender), it is tempting to think that we can spend a year reading books on that topic to find a perspective that works for us, apart from consulting our community. It is important to note the tendency for humans to want to make theological decisions apart from the local church.

In our time, as Western Christians are imbued with such strong individualist tendencies, it is incumbent on us to always seek to drive ourselves back to community to make decisions together. Paul, in his first letter to the church in Corinth, outlines clear and concise directions for the life of the church. But he ends his teaching in 1 Corinthians 11 by writing, "And when I come I will give further directions" (v. 34). Paul was willing to offer the most essential ideas. But there were evidently other instructions he would share only when he was *with* the church in Corinth. When we read the New Testament, we are giving these voices of church history the first opportunity to speak as we do theology together.

A Painful Lesson

A few years ago we learned the painful lesson of doing theology too quickly—and doing it alone. Just before the release of A. J.'s book *After Doubt*, which navigates the realities of those experiencing doubt and deconstruction, we wrote an article that was to be published in a major Christian magazine. The article wondered if Jesus, as a true human, experienced the full realities of existential angst and doubt on the cross. Did he actually mean what he said when he quoted Psalm 22: "My God, my God, why have you forsaken me?" (v. 1).

It was our conviction that by showing Christ—fully human and fully God—in his most painful moment of despair, it could offer hope to those walking through their own despairing doubt. We published the piece on Good Friday, just before Easter, and were hopeful that it would provide solace to countless people wrestling with their own painful moments. What happened deeply surprised us. Our article went viral. But not the way we wished it to. Thousands of tweets later, for the better part of three days, we were cast aside for considering whether Jesus himself experienced doubt. The experience was deeply painful for both of us. One of us had to be put on medication. The other experienced such deep distress that he had to be admitted to the emergency room for heart palpitations.

Thankfully, people are very distracted. And the story disappeared after just a couple of days. But the experience left a mark on both of us. While the thrust of the argument still stands as valid in our minds, we left the experience the wiser. What did we learn?

We made two critical errors. First, we wrote the article in a day's time and posted it immediately. While quick turnarounds are normal for most people who publish their work, in hindsight we believe we had *too* quick a turnaround. Were we to write it again, we would have given more time and space to thinking through our overall argument and the ramifications of some of our language.

Second, we failed to have our draft reviewed by individuals we know and trust before hitting send. Both of us have deep, enriching, and life-giving relationships with people who know their stuff in the academy. We are also deeply connected to people on the ground in churches. One of the lessons we learned was that the work of theology necessitates community—and including the voices of people who can help us see our blind spots is of utmost importance. Truth be told, we doubt that many of the individuals we wish we had consulted beforehand would have changed much of the article's substance. But perhaps they would have. And the argument would only have been sharper.

Humans are communal beings. We are as good as the community that surrounds us. One should not be surprised in the least when they see a young person go off to college, leave their church, find themselves in a whole new environment, and go through major changes in their faith. In fact, it is often in moving away from the communities and environments that have shaped us that we tend to make massive theological shifts.[11] We tend to reflect the theology of the community we rely on.

Part of being a deeply formed person is learning to lean on those communities. We will all lean on something or someone in times of need. The question is, *Who* do we lean on?

With One Voice

What we say together has the power to shape us. Forty-seven of the fifty states in the United States require that the Pledge of Allegiance be recited each day (or at least often) in public schools—hand on

157

heart, together with one voice, and usually memorized. Many who grew up reciting the national creed got used to it; it was simply something they had to do during the day in school, and not much thought was put into it. But when we grow up and enter adult life, something begins to change. The communal statements tend to, well, disappear. Have you ever thought about that? You might encounter such statements occasionally at some sporting events or civic ceremonies, but in daily life a community reciting something aloud together just doesn't happen much anywhere in our culture. That is, *except in church*. Not all churches, of course, but some (often mainline, Catholic, or liturgical) have creeds and confessions that are publicly voiced and affirmed by the congregation.

In the past, most evangelicals have been wary of these kinds of corporate confessions out of fear that they might come across as forced, impersonal, or just plain dull. But lately, the phenomenon of publicly reciting a creed has been making a surge among folks who otherwise might be known as "low church." There have been numerous studies on this phenomenon, but part of the reason behind its resurgence is a stronger connection to the global and historic church and a sense of unity with the ancient beliefs and teachings of the faith.[12] And certainly another component is the embodied practice of standing together and using our voices willfully and actively.

It's as though we crave shared beliefs.

It is healthy for a community to say in unison out loud what they believe and value. A historic Christian creed not only allows us to say what we believe but also shapes us by hearing one another saying the same things. Luke Timothy Johnson, who has written one of the most important books on the subject (simply called *The Creed*), makes the case that reciting our faith together using historical statements helps believers reinforce a certain way of looking at the world, over and against other ways. Johnson says that creeds (like the Apostles' Creed) reinforce "a specifically Christian conception of reality."[13] Johnson's characteristic eloquence is on full display in his breakdown of how Christians who verbally and communally confess the faith establish a resilient worldview together:

> In a world that celebrates individuality, they are actually doing something together. In an age that avoids commitment, they pledge themselves to a set of convictions and thereby to each other. In a culture that rewards novelty and creativity, they use words written by others long ago. In a society where accepted wisdom changes by the minute, they claim that some truths are so critical that they must be repeated over and over again. In a throwaway, consumerist world, they accept, preserve, and continue tradition. Reciting the creed at worship is thus a countercultural act.[14]

The origins of the Christian creeds go back to the early church, where the early Apostles' Creed began with the Latin word *credo*, which literally means "I believe." But we have to be careful not to import a modern sense of individualism on this "I." This creed was first confessed after a believer made a serious commitment to the faith and was baptized. This "I" confession represented personal participation in the community. As we integrate into a faith community, the individual "I" morphs into a communal "I," an "I" that is actually the body of Christ speaking as one. The creed does not reflect the truth of our faith based simply on what each of us believes individually. Our personal faith is always in flux. Most of us live our whole lives in the state of the man in Mark 9 who said to Jesus, "I do believe; help me overcome my unbelief!" (v. 24). None of us believe perfectly all by ourselves, but the creeds are not about individuals who profess faith in the same room as other believers.

Theologian Ben Myers reminds us that professing the faith may involve saying "I believe," but it is in fact a "we" dynamic. (In fact, many denominations have adapted the creeds to start with "We believe . . .") Myers expresses that when we verbalize the creed in a congregation of believers, we join "a community stretched out across history, 'terrible as an army with banners' (Song 6:10)."[15] It is as if our words help us become grafted into the deep roots of the church that has been alive and growing for two thousand years and counting. We are touching the past to better understand the present. "That gives us critical distance from our own time and place," Myers explains. "If our voices are still echoes, they are now echoing something from beyond our own cultural moment."[16]

The Danger of Extremes

Theologically, we must make room as individuals *and* as a community to think about God. We desperately need both. There are times when the community is right and the individual needs to be corrected. This is one of the most important aspects of living in a community larger than ourselves. To be in the church is to open yourself up to correction and rebuke—something we all desperately need. It is endlessly comforting for us to know that we live in communities that would lovingly confront us and hold us to the character and truths of Christ. Without that community, we are bound to do whatever we wish.

There are also times when the community needs to be corrected by the individual. In fact, this is the very history of the Protestant tradition. Protestantism began as a story of a quiet monk named Martin Luther nailing ninety-five statements and questions on a door in Wittenberg, Germany. Luther saw the toxicity and abuse in the church. And he needed to speak out against it. While he would be banned as a heretic, the movement that followed him would become what we know as Protestantism. We would both agree that many of Luther's calls to reform were needed corrections. Ironically, though Luther was ousted from the Roman Catholic Church, many of the reforms he proposed would be enacted years later in the Council of Trent between 1545 and 1563. This would be called the Counter-Reformation.

The tension between the community and the individual is one that plays out time and again in church history. Oftentimes the pendulum swings in the extremes. Some communities in Christian history have, we would argue, *over*emphasized the place of community to the degree that the individual does not matter anymore. Think radical Amish communities, where the personality of the individual is largely muted by the communal identity. Other communities do the opposite—everything is about the individual. The faith is individualized, accepted by a person alone, all by oneself.

This kind of individualized approach to faith may explain why we are seeing so many individuals raised in evangelical churches convert to Roman Catholicism and Eastern Orthodoxy. If we have been raised in entirely individualistic environments, we come to recognize, down the road, that we need something that goes beyond ourselves. We come to long for a faith that is not dependent on my opinions on a matter or what I personally believe. So we turn to communities in which the faith is the faith of the community.

Perhaps a way to think about this is to consider the nature of the Trinity. In historic Christian teaching, God is one *ousia* ("being") and three *persona* ("persons"). This teaching has been handed down for two thousand years and is inseparable from recognizable, global Christianity.

Of course, the Trinity is difficult to understand. Rightly so. It is a mystery. The rational mind does not know what to do with it. So it seeks to make it more understandable and rational. We hear this in the words of the founding father Thomas Jefferson, who was a deist: "The Trinity is incomprehensible jargon and arithmetic that three are one. We must therefore return to a simple faith."[17] For Jefferson, the Trinity was simply too cumbersome and irrational to be believed. The church, he believed, must return to the "simple faith." That is always the call of heresy—to return to simplicity. This can be seen in almost all the early heresies of the early church. The heretics argued either that there was one God who simply presented as different persons (modalism) or, worse yet, that there were three different gods who functioned as a triad of power (essentially a form of polytheism). These responses reveal something about the unsanctified human mind. When it encounters mystery, it always yearns for something easy and simple.

Good theology, though, never simplifies mystery. Theology embraces what is true because it is true—not because it makes complete sense. The nature of the Trinity is deeply formative for our theological reflection. The Trinity guards two things. First, it guards the unity of God—that is, the three persons of the Father, Son, and Holy Spirit are actually one in purpose, love, and mission. They are one in a relationship. But, second, the Trinity guards the distinct personality of each person in the Godhead. They are actually three different persons with their own personality. The Father, Spirit, and Son are singularly unique.

Like the Trinity, to do theology well is to embrace simultaneously the communal and individual nature of the truth.

DON'T EVER GIVE UP

Those Who Make It to the End Will Win

The Long Race

If someone finds themselves near Thomas Edison Technical High School in the Jamaica neighborhood of Queens, New York, they might witness one of the most incredible events taking place in the United States that almost nobody has heard of or paid attention to: the 3100 Mile Race. Yes, you read that correctly—3,100 miles! Since 1996, select ultramarathon runners have been invited to this neighborhood each summer to compete in a race around a single city block. In total, they will run around this one block 5,500 times over about 50 days. Competitors run from 6 a.m. until midnight, covering approximately 60 miles per day.

The world champion of the race is a Finnish man named Ashprihanal Aalto. In one of his thirteen participations in the 3100 Mile Race, he broke the record, finishing in 40 days, 9 hours, 6 minutes, and 21 seconds. His time beat the previous record by nearly an entire day. Now, the big question everyone asks is, Why? Why would anyone want to spend almost two months of their life running in circles?

Unlike other races, this one is not about the money. Some races, like the Boston Marathon, offer participants the chance to win six-figure prizes. Not in the Jamaica neighborhood of Queens. There is no prize—other than a T-shirt and a plastic trophy. That's it. Participants in this race are motivated by something different. It's not about fame or fortune. The 3100 Mile Race is a test of personal endurance, determination, and grit. Many competitors even describe it as a "spiritual experience," which is why the race is officially known as the Self-Transcendence 3100 Mile Race.

The idea for the race was conceived by Chinmoy Kumar Ghose (1931–2007), who sought to promote athleticism as a pathway to a deep inner spiritual journey. Ghose wanted people to learn how to train their inner person so they could thrive in their everyday lives. Those who complete the race—and not everyone does—come knowing that they are facing a battle that is just as much mental and spiritual as it is physical. Can they train themselves to overcome pain, exhaustion, fear, and even boredom to achieve the seemingly impossible? Underneath this challenge lies a deep belief that many people struggle with life's difficulties because they haven't trained their inner selves to overcome exhaustion, pain, and tedium.

Most people will not have the ability in their lifetime to compete in the 3100 Mile Race. But everyone can learn a critical lesson about the purpose and mission of the spiritual life of following Jesus. The Christian race is a difficult one. Maybe this is one of the reasons that we are watching the proliferation of the "dones" (those who claim to be "done" with the Christian journey) in the Western church. Many, it seems, were probably never taught that challenges, setbacks, and obstacles are the *norm*, not the exception. To be able to finish this race, you can't simply buy some new shoes, show up, and hope for the best. This kind of journey requires the cultivation of determination, commitment, endurance, and grit. Too many evangelists preach an easy faith to "win" more believers. But the way of Jesus is not easy; it's hard. Jesus does respond quickly and generously when he gives grace to those who know their sin and their desperate need for a Savior. The response time between raising your hand to ask for help and Jesus rushing to your side is instantaneous. But then the journey of transformation begins, and it is more than 3,100 miles.

The need for these qualities of determination and perseverance was something Jesus consistently instructed his disciples about. For example, as Jesus sends out his Twelve into the mission field for the first time (Matt. 10:1–40), one of the first things he intentionally does is instruct them about the very real danger of enemies and deceivers—what he calls "sheep among wolves" (v. 16). Jesus further tells them that they will be arrested, paraded around, interrogated, beaten; there will be temptation to betray each other, and the faithful will be openly mocked and hated: "But the one who stands firm to the end will be saved" (v. 22).

A simple perusal of Jesus's teachings in the Gospels will reveal time and again that he understood the pathway of discipleship to be one marked by hardship, persecution, difficulty, and suffering. To follow Jesus, it seems, was a one-way ticket to martyrdom. Yikes! Of course, all that pain and difficulty was far from futile. The silver lining is that it is worth it in the end, which is why it is so important that we persevere. According to Matthew's Gospel, Jesus gave an important teaching on this just before the Last Supper and his arrest. He warned the disciples that they must be vigilant, because the days of chaos and anarchy are coming, and enemies will hate Jesus's people and put them to death. This will lead to fear and terror, and many will betray one another and fall away from their faith, but "the one who stands firm to the end will be saved" (24:13).

Jesus's repeated emphasis on endurance and perseverance invites the question, Who will remain faithful when the going gets rough? Who has the mettle and determination to do what most people cannot do? Jesus was very clear with his disciples that the choice to follow him was a decision to walk a hard road, not an easy one. In fact, it would be the hardest road imaginable, and, frankly, *many* would give up. We learn a sobering lesson from a first-century Christian named Demas. He was, at one time, a passionate Christian who was a church leader and a close friend of Luke (the physician and Gospel writer) and the apostle Paul (Col. 4:14; Philem. v. 24). But in one of Paul's final letters (his second letter to Timothy) he writes this: "Do your best to come to me quickly, for Demas, because he loved this world, has deserted me" (2 Tim. 4:9–10). These are heartbreaking words that Paul must have written with immense grief. We don't know if Demas ever turned his life back around, but if this is the end of the story, then Demas did not prepare himself for the difficult race of faith. He saw an enticing exit and took it.

There are likely many reasons we are seeing an increase in the "dones" leaving the church. Not all of it can be attributed to a lack of discipline, fortitude, and perseverance. But if the Gospels tell us that many of the people who followed Jesus from the beginning were not in it for the long haul, we can be assured that the same will happen in our own time. In a culture that seeks comfort and happiness, who would want cross and crucifixion? Dietrich Bonhoeffer poignantly expounds this concept in his famous book *The Cost of Discipleship*:

> Suffering . . . is the badge of true discipleship. The disciple is not above his master. Following Christ means *passio passiva*, suffering because we have to suffer. . . . If we refuse to take up our cross and submit to suffering and rejection at the hands of men, we forfeit our fellowship with Christ and have ceased to follow him. But if we lose our lives in his service and carry our cross, we shall find our lives again in the fellowship of the cross with Christ.[1]

Perseverance Practicalities

There are numerous parallels between the ambitions of a runner (like that in the 3100 Mile Race) and a disciple of Jesus Christ. No doubt, we have something to learn about perseverance, determination, planning, and grit from such athletes. Ultimately these runners are asking themselves, How can I persevere to the end in a seemingly impossible race with challenges that are both predictable and unpredictable? Followers of Jesus are asking the same questions because Jesus taught us to ask them. How do I prepare myself—mind, body, and spirit—to follow Jesus through the ups and down, rain or shine?

The reality is that there is no magic formula for how to persevere in the faith in the long run. What we learn from Jesus in the Gospels is that knowing what we're in for ahead of time is an important preparation for hardships, setbacks, and low points. Jesus's encouragement to his disciples was that sticking with the gospel and the way of Jesus really is worth it if you are willing to stay committed for the long haul. Many fall away simply because they cannot appreciate the benefit that goes along with the cost. But as with Bonhoeffer, we must recognize the *cost* of discipleship, and in the end that the cost is worth it, because we are given much more than we could have ever imagined.

When Jesus taught the disciples about losing everything to gain more through *him*, he said, "Truly I tell you, at the renewal of all things, when the Son of Man sits on his glorious throne, you who have followed me will also sit on twelve thrones, judging the twelve tribes of Israel. And everyone who has left houses or brothers or sisters or father or mother or wife or children or fields for my sake will receive a hundred times as much and will inherit eternal life" (Matt. 19:28–29). The key is making it to the end. It's like the old "Hands on a Hardbody" contest that started in Texas in the 1990s but became a popular trend throughout the 1990s and early 2000s. Basically, a car dealership runs a contest where whoever enters has to be touching the car with their hand around the clock (with a few previously agreed-on breaks for personal needs), and the last person still touching the car wins it. Typically, dozens of people start out, thinking they could win. One by one, they give up due to exhaustion, accidental rule-breaking, or sheer boredom. *Who's willing to stick it out until the end?*

While there is no clear silver bullet for persevering in your faith until the end, there is plenty of wisdom that can be applied to a "long obedience in the same direction"[2] (as Eugene Peterson so memorably borrowed from Nietzsche). Ultramarathoners who have participated in the 3100 Mile Race have shared the advice that has helped them achieve what appears to be the impossible, and much of this advice is relevant for longevity of faith, hope, and love in Christ Jesus. In what follows we adapt their advice for the faith journey.

1. Pace yourself.

Veterans of the 3100 Mile Race often tell a cautionary tale of a running athlete who was new to ultramarathons and bit off more than he could chew. He started out trying to run seventy miles a day (putting him on track for a forty-four-day finish, versus a newcomer's more typical goal of fifty-two days). He felt great the first few days, but after a heat wave struck New York, this ambitious racer dropped out, not even making it to the end of week one. Making it in the long run requires thinking ahead, setting a challenging but sustainable pace. For our faith, we need to develop good habits that will last over the long haul—communing with God and others, reading Scripture, participating in acts of service and generosity, but all the while planning for decades of strong faith (knowing the "heat waves" are inevitable).

2. Find joy in the struggle.

The 3100 Mile Race experts have all learned one thing intimately: The pain will come. Swollen feet, shin splints, blisters, and plenty of aches. (Runners of this unique race burn through ten to fifteen pairs of shoes when all is said and done.)[3] If you are trying to avoid physical pain, you are in the wrong race. Part of the spirituality of ultramarathon running is adjusting to pain and even finding joy in the predictability of it, knowing everyone else is going through it, and trusting that this is simply what is experienced on the way to something greater. It can be easy, in our Christian spirituality, to pray for and seek out freedom from pain, including emotional, social, and spiritual hurt. But it is woven so seamlessly into the human experience that we have to accept that it's just part of life. The decision is whether we ignore it, run from it, or expect it and have a plan for treating and healing from it.

3. Celebrate today's small victories and blessings.

Successful long-distance runners have to think both about the whole race (beginning to end) and the smaller goals. Even trying to imagine completing a 3,100-mile race is daunting, especially the first time a runner decides to do it. It seems impossible. But breaking it up into smaller pieces and celebrating little victories (like a few laps completed or a successful day) keeps spirits high. With Jesus, it's all about finding gratitude and signs of God's presence and blessing each and every day, even on cloudy days, and especially on the hardest days.

4. Resting makes us stronger.

Athletes understand the science of rest. Decorated Olympic runner Bernard Lagat has a yearly practice of taking a five-week break from running.[4] In his normal training routine, he might aim to run more than eighty miles in a week, but during this extended rest period, he enjoys hobbies, eats good food, and takes it easy. He knows that this is necessary to prevent burnout and helps him to look forward to running again. There is also the reality of stress relief. Taking rest allows the body, mind, and soul to relax.

Americans overall, and Christian leaders in particular, are actually very bad at rest. There is a rat-race mentality that takes control
and prevents cycles of healthy rest and rejuvenation. This can
easily lead to burnout, overwhelming stress, and even depression.
The only sensible solution is building into life both frequent short
periods of rest and occasional longer periods of rest.

5. Fill up on the right foods.

Running all day, every day for over a month requires a lot of
calories per day—10,000 calories, according to veteran runners.
And it can't be chips and soda. It matters *what* you eat—namely,
the most nutrient-rich and energy-rich foods that will sustain the
runners for the long haul. It is the same with the Christian faith.
What we put into our minds and hearts and bodies will make a
huge difference in our spiritual health. Are we listening to trusted
teachers for our theological instruction; seeking out mentorship
from wise, mature believers; and focusing on God's Word? Or are
we letting cynical or anti-Christian voices flood our ears?

In Need of a Team Sport

One of the gifts of this race is that we do not do it alone. When
Paul commands Christians to run the race, he gives them this
commandment in the context of community. Each of us must
run in the race, but we don't run all on our own. Many sports
are individual sports. When someone watches an Olympic sport
such as gymnastics, they are watching an individual perform a
routine or skill that they have worked on for decades. While the
practice and the formation may have taken place with the help
of many coaches and colaborers, the performance itself is done
individually.

Other Olympic sporting events are communal. Think basket-
ball, volleyball, soccer, water polo, and field hockey. These sports
are composed of a team of individuals who work together to win

their event. One such event is the medley relay in swimming. Here, four swimmers share the race by each giving their all in one particular style of swimming—backstroke, freestyle, breaststroke, and butterfly. Each style requires a different kind of expertise and skill set. But together, the four individuals are able to do the race in hopes of coming in with the best overall time.

It would be easy to project much of our individualist culture on the biblical story.[5] Too often, we read the story of the Bible as a series of individual performances rather than the whole story of the community. We see this, for example, in the narrative of Joshua when the people of God are crossing over the River Jordan into the promised land. God wanted all the people to cross into the land of deliverance. But some tribes decided they were going to finally settle on the east side of the Jordan. The tribes of Reuben and Gad and the half tribe of Manasseh wanted to build their camps on the side of the Jordan that they saw could sustain their livestock. God blessed their desire. And, in Numbers 32, Moses eventually gave them permission to do so.

Under one caveat. They had to help the other tribes cross over Jordan first. Then they could return to the land that they saw could sustain their community. The entire story is framed in the context of a community. If everyone does not finish the race to the promised land, then nobody gets to. God deeply desires that the entirety of his people should enter the rest that had been promised all the way back to Moses's calling in Exodus 3.

Paul calls us to run the race. But we run this race with others. This is both good and painful. It is good because it means that we do it together. We run together. We walk together. We struggle together. We celebrate together. The race is a race that is to be run as an entire community. It is painful in that it slows us down. Being open to taking the journey slower than we may be able to do on our own requires that we take on an entirely new perspective toward perseverance. God doesn't just reward finishing the race. God also rewards us for finishing the race *together*.

One of the important developments in theology over the past few decades has been the emergence of much-needed conversation around disability. How should God's people think about how they make space for and create environments that welcome and nurture the spiritual lives of all—including those who are not able-bodied? When we begin to think about those who are not neurotypical or experience bodily difficulty, it reframes everything about how we approach the work of doing church. If a church does not have wheelchair access for a person coming forward to receive communion, what does this say about its theology of God's grace and mercy? When the teaching of a church connects only with the way a neurotypical person thinks, what does it say about the church's understanding of the gospel?

Asking these kinds of questions is central, but it does slow things down. Whenever a church goes through a building campaign or moves toward buying a church building, questions like these add to the complexity of the project. But they are questions that deserve to be asked. Why? Because the way in which we approach these questions speaks to our deepest theological commitments. That is, how we run the race with others exposes the deepest things that we believe about God. If we do not take the time to consider these realities because they get in the way of "mission," then our theology of mission is exposed. How often do we care about God's mission only to the degree that it impacts people whose bodies look like ours? If we do not think about the minds and brains of people who don't fit the mold of normativity, then our theology of the gospel has been laid bare.

The slowest person in any church is almost always the one who exposes the theology of that church. We should see that person who may be slower than the rest as the one who brings us near to the heart of Christ. The church has a gospel obligation to listen carefully to the cries, words, and whimpers of those who experience daily in their body the difficulty of brokenness. Our problem is that we are in a hurry and don't take time to listen.

Henri Nouwen left his life in the academy and spent years serving individuals with disabilities. He wrote a book about one such young man he served and named it after him: *Adam*. Adam's communication was limited. And he was almost impossible to understand. After being diagnosed as deaf, he was fitted with hearing aids. He was not comforted, and he kept ripping them off. Time and time again, people put the hearing aids back on only to find them torn off within minutes.

Only after some time did people realize that Adam was not deaf at all. He had been wrongly diagnosed. The hearing aids were not helping a deaf person hear, they were amplifying sounds for a man who could hear—the pain of which was unbearable. Later, Adam's father lamented, "I think he suffered so much, but we never knew because he could not tell us."[6]

In an individualist culture like our own, we diagnose individuals who slow us down as problems. In reality they are the cure for our individualism. The race needs to be run. But if we run it all alone, what is the use of running?

It might seem like everything we are calling for in this chapter, perhaps in this book, sounds like a great burden. We need to be slow sometimes, fast at other times; we need to balance opposites and hold on to tensions tightly; we need to learn how to run the long race and not give up; we need to gain dexterity at working together as a group. How can anyone have the skills, knowledge, energy, and fortune to accomplish all these things? We can't, and if we try to do it by sheer grit and bootstrapping it, we'll get burned out. Thankfully, Jesus gave us the key to accomplishing all of this in some of his final teachings before his crucifixion. He taught us the most important verb, "abide."

The Disciple Abides

The Gospel of John is sometimes called the "maverick" Gospel. John shows the story of Jesus in a unique way from his brothers

Matthew, Mark, and Luke. As a result, the reader encounters a variety of stories in John that are found nowhere else, which gives the book its distinctive style. John, for example, does not include a single parable. But at the same time, he is the only apostle to tell the story of the miracle in Cana (John 2:1–13) and the washing of the disciples' feet (13:1–18). Some of the more memorable teachings of Jesus are found only in John, such as "I am the way and the truth and the life" (14:6), and "For God so loved the world" (3:16), and "I have come that they may have life, and have it to the full" (10:10). And there is the classic vine and branches teaching, which is best read in the King James Version (with a proper British accent; we like to imagine Sir David Attenborough's voice):

> Abide in me, and I in you. As the branch cannot bear fruit of itself, except it abide in the vine; no more can ye, except ye abide in me. I am the vine, ye are the branches: He that abideth in me, and I in him, the same bringeth forth much fruit: for without me ye can do nothing. (15:4)

It sounds good in a church service Bible reading, but most Christians don't stop to really reflect on the theological meaning of the verb "abide." After all, we don't use it in day-to-day conversation. "Abide" has a kind of old-timey religious ring to it; it sounds holy and spiritual (and it's used in the cult classic *The Big Lebowski* in the saying, "The dude abides"). "Abide" sounds like a transcendent state of being and spiritual bond with the divine that is otherworldly and mysterious, doesn't it? So it is a little ironic that the Greek word that John uses here is *menō*, a very common and ordinary word for living, persisting, or remaining in one place. In fact, its most basic meaning is "to stay."

The same verb is used at the very beginning of John, when two of John the Baptist's disciples pursue Jesus and ask, "Where are you staying [*menō*]?" (1:38). There's nothing especially spiritual or mystical about their question. They just want to know where he's going to be later on. "Come," Jesus replies, "and you will see" (1:39). Go and see, and stay with him for a while, John tells us. Now, if you are reading John for the first time, and you read that these disciples stuck around for a day or so, it doesn't seem like a big deal. But as you read on, this turns out to be what discipleship is all about in John's Gospel. It's not a set of activities to accomplish or spiritual disciplines to master. It's about hanging out with Jesus, *menō-ing*, remaining, staying, abiding. The Samaritans come to Jesus and ask him to stay with them, so he does. He *menō-s* for two days (4:40). When Jesus teaches on belonging to the great household of God, he distinguishes between a slave and a permanent member of the family—the slave doesn't have a right to stay, but the children do; they can stay forever and ever, and Jesus wants everyone to be children who know they have an eternal home with God (8:35).

We come to learn from John's Gospel that abiding is not religious mumbo jumbo; the theological importance of abiding is that eternal life and lasting human fulfillment are about finding a home and resting place with God here and now. "Remain [*menō*] in my love," Jesus commands his disciples (15:9). What a weird command! But it makes more sense if we interpret it this way: "Make yourself at home in my household of love forever."

When Jesus teaches, "Abide in me, and I in you," it's a simple concept: "Let's take the time to slow down, to be together, to focus on each other, to live life together." Too many churches today focus on methods and tools, as if knowing God involves doing all the right things in the exact right way to get the right results. That can easily lead to a false sense of superiority for those "good" Christians who seem so spiritual; for too many others, it leads to guilt, shame, and discouragement. For the latter, John's Gospel can be a healing message about what God really wants: not *doing more* for the sake of impressing God but rather putting yourself in the right place (in the presence of Jesus) and just being there, staying, remaining—*abiding*. That's Christianity at its most basic: yearning to be near Christ and to do whatever it is that he is doing. And he wants the same, to be near us.

The capacity to abide is, for the author of the letter to the Hebrews, the definition of a follower of Christ. Hebrews says, "We have come to share in Christ, if indeed we hold our original conviction firmly to the very end" (3:14). There is perhaps no clearer definition in all the New Testament about what a Christian actually is. A Christian is not someone who fleetingly believes for a year and then moves on to the next best thing. The Christian—the one who abides in Jesus—is the one who continues to hold firmly to their love for Christ until their very end. This is the work of long-suffering and perseverance. It is the task of putting our full identity, call, and life in the hands of Christ and choosing to never let go.

One of our colleagues, Dan Brunner, has shown us what this kind of faithfulness can be like. Over the course of nearly a decade, Dan's wife Signey withered away under a cancer diagnosis. She eventually died on a Good Friday. Dan spent years caring for his wife, feeding her, loving her, bending his life around her every need. In the most powerful of ways, this is the abiding kind of love that we are called to embody. We are called by God to stay, to stick, to love Jesus to the very end—even if it costs us tremendously.

CONCLUSION

Perplext in faith, but pure in deeds,
At last he beat his music out.
There lives more faith in honest doubt,
Believe me, than in half the creeds.

He fought his doubts and gather'd strength,
He would not make his judgment blind,
He faced the spectres of the mind
And laid them: thus he came at length

To find a stronger faith his own;
And Power was with him in the night,
Which makes the darkness and the light,
And dwells not in the light alone
        —Alfred Tennyson,
        "In Memoriam A. H. H."[1]

The challenge of any chaotic moment is to not lose touch with the voice of Jesus. To follow Christ is to seek endlessly to hear the voice of the Savior. We all can lose touch with the most important voices. In Genesis 27, we're told the story of Isaac approaching his death.

Near the end of his life, he wants to bless the older son, Esau. He tells Esau to go out and catch some game so that they can enjoy a meal for the blessing ceremony. But listening is Rebekah, Isaac's wife. She favors Jacob, the younger son, so she tells him of Isaac's plan. She sends him out before Esau can go to catch some game, then has Jacob enter in and deceive Isaac, who can no longer see.

As Jacob enters in with his kill, Isaac feels his hand. He then says, "The voice is the voice of Jacob, but the hands are the hands of Esau" (Gen. 27:22). What this intimate story narrates for us is the experience of a father who, in his last days, is being torn between his knowledge of his son's voice and the feeling of his other son's hands. Isaac knew what Jacob's voice sounded like. He also knew what Esau's hands felt like. Something was off. What we are beholding is the experience of a father who'd spent his life learning the sound of his son's voice. Voices must be learned, discerned, and recognized. We come to know the voice of the beloved.

Jesus often taught his disciples about his own voice. In the Gospel of John, Jesus tells his disciples that they will be people who could recognize his voice. They would know what his voice sounds like:

> The sheep listen to his voice. He calls his own sheep by name and leads them out. When he has brought out all his own, he goes on ahead of them, and his sheep follow him because they know his voice. But they will never follow a stranger; in fact, they will run away from him because they do not recognize a stranger's voice. (John 10:3–5)

A voice is learned over time. But we must continue listening to that voice, never losing touch with it.

We have turned to Augustine several times throughout this book, and we can do no better than to conclude with more wisdom from the brilliant bishop of Hippo. In one letter correspondence (Letter 93), Augustine was asked by a colleague how much someone should push and prod to move someone from heresy to the truth. The Christian, it was accepted, was called at all times to gentleness. But when should they take a stronger approach, be more firm, and even use a heavy hand?

Without any sense of hesitation, Augustine exhorts his friend not to shy away from strong words and actions toward correction. Augustine was not trying to condone bullying, violence, or theological arrogance. Rather, he was reflecting on how he himself had needed to be disciplined by God when he was living wrongly. God disciplines us. And sometimes we need discipline from one another. After experiencing God's loving correction, Augustine believed that God's firm hand—like the shepherd who has to use the guiding rod to keep the sheep in line for their own safety—would lead anyone back to God.

In this conversation (and in many others), Augustine repeatedly uses a phrase that relates to the importance of discipline in the Christian life: *eruditio per molestias*, "learning through hardships." Augustine was quick to explain in his letter that God gives us trials and difficulties not because he likes to watch us suffer. He does it because we need to learn how to want the good and reject the bad. Augustine explains that Scripture testifies of a God who allowed the patriarchs to suffer famines in order to increase their faith, who had to discipline Israel's rebellion in the wilderness to lead them to the promised land, and who refused to answer Paul's constant prayers for the removal of his thorn in the flesh so that he might be perfected through weakness. Augustine concludes that just as we praise gifts and blessings from God, we need to recognize his love in the hard stuff.

The reality Scripture teaches us is that while it is fundamentally true that we are saved by grace, not by works—we live only by the mercy and love of God, and we can't earn his goodwill—it is also true that each one of us has a journey to complete from day one toward the wholeness we are destined for, *per molestias*, through many trials, tribulations, and hardships. We aren't alone.

We live by abiding in Christ through the Spirit. We are given a great company of fellow pilgrims in the church. But we can't stand still. This book, we hope, has been a kind of "survivor's guide" to the Christian journey, a dangerous path that many have attempted unprepared.

James says to his readers that they should "consider it pure joy . . . whenever you face trials of many kinds" (James 1:2). Not all trials are the same. Some trials are the little hardships from a normal day like losing your keys, getting a mean email, or being frustrated with something in politics. Other trials prove to be bigger hardships: losing a job because of fidelity to the way of Jesus, seeing a family member turn away from their faith, or, in some situations, actual embodied persecutions. There are, indeed, "trials of many kinds." But in all of them we should consider it pure joy.

Why? Because all these things are making us into deeper, more formed, and more authentic human beings.

May you, the reader, keep your ears attuned to the voice of the Lamb. As you do, hear his heart, his love, and his care for you. These are turbulent times. But God is always ready to be heard.

Stay faithful.

ACKNOWLEDGMENTS

This book comes out of the fruitful work that A. J. and I have been doing with our podcast by the same name, *Slow Theology*. I want to thank A. J. for his book *After Doubt*, which was the inspiration for the podcast, and I also want to thank A. J. for his friendship, which has been a joy and a blessing these many years we have lived in Oregon together. I would like to thank my wife Amy for modeling a deep life of prayer and a passionate pursuit of Christ. I would also like to acknowledge the devoted listeners of our podcast who have sent us emails and messages with great questions, helpful feedback, and encouraging comments.

On the publication of this book, we extend our appreciation to editor and friend Bob Hosack and the excellent team at Brazos. Their work was done slowly, carefully, and with excellence. Finally, I want to thank our readers, who chose to pick up this book to inspire their own faith or the faith of others. Our deepest desire is that in the churning sea storms of life, people will squint their eyes and see the beacon of Christ lighting the way.

Nijay K. Gupta

There's an old saying: A theologian is someone who's happy when more people read their work than wrote it. If you're reading this, then I guess we are successful theologians in some regard. The truth remains that the singular mark of a good and true theologian has little (if anything) to do with the size of their readership. In the Christian story, a good theologian first and foremost opts to think about God with a heart and mind of love for the God on which they reflect. Good theologians don't write for the numbers. They write as doxology. Of course, no theologian worth their salt can undertake their work alone. They are forged and founded in a community of people who help them do what they do—holding up their arms as they type just as Aaron and Hur held up Moses's hands as he prayed (Exod. 17:12).

I would like to thank the people who have held up my hands. I have four public acknowledgments I wish to make. First, Quinn and Elliot, you have held up my arms the most. Second, Nijay, you have become one of my closest friends and allies. I love serving the church with you. Third, it is worth acknowledging the one who helped me take my first theological steps—Dr. Mark Cartledge. You were an incredible *doktorvater*. I would not be doing what I do without your care and support. Finally, I wish to acknowledge two pastors: Steve Overman and Nate Poetzl. For years, I sat under both of your pastoral wisdom and guidance. As shepherds of two congregations of which I've had the privilege to sit, you were the ones who taught me firsthand the virtue of slowing down to hear God's voice in pastoral leadership. I'm deeply grateful for your hands upon my life. It is my hope that this next season of life brings you nothing but the joy of grace, knowing that you have done your work faithfully and steadily.

A. J. Swoboda

NOTES

Foreword

1. Abbott Kahler, "The Daredevil of Niagara Falls," *Smithsonian Magazine*, October 18, 2011, https://www.smithsonianmag.com/history/the-daredevil-of -niagara-falls-110492884.

Introduction

1. Frederick Buechner, *Beyond Words: Daily Readings in the ABC's of Faith* (HarperSanFrancisco, 2004), 43.

2. *Theophrastus Paracelsus: Werke*, vol. 2 (Wissenschaftliche Buchgesellschaft, 1965), 509.

3. J. R. R. Tolkien, *The Fellowship of the Ring* (George Allen & Unwin, 1966), 60.

4. On this phenomenon, begin with A. J. Swoboda, *After Doubt: How to Question Your Faith Without Losing It* (Brazos, 2020).

5. Nassim Nicholas Taleb, *Antifragile: Things That Gain from Disorder* (Random House, 2014).

6. Taleb, *Antifragile*, 5.

7. Stuart Murray, *Post-Christendom: Church and Mission in a Strange New World*, 2nd ed. (Cascade, 2018), chap. 2.

8. Jean-Dominique Bauby, *The Diving Bell and the Butterfly* (Knopf Doubleday, 2008).

Chapter 1 Take Your Time

1. Wesley's dual commitment to Scripture and scientific knowledge would eventually form what is called the Wesleyan quadrilateral. For two helpful introductions to this tradition, see Thomas Oden and Leicester Longden, *The Wesleyan Theological Heritage: Essays of Albert C. Outler* (Zondervan, 1991); and Donald Thorsen, *The Wesleyan Quadrilateral: Scripture, Tradition, Reason and Experience as a Model of Evangelical Theology* (Zondervan, 1990).

2. John Wesley, *The Works of the Rev. John Wesley* (London: J. Mason, 1856), 6:198.

3. Though it's unclear where in Wesley's writings this line is derived, it nonetheless captures the spirit of Wesley's awe. J. Vernon McGee, *Thru the Bible with J. Vernon McGee: Genesis–Deuteronomy* (Thru the Bible Radio, 1981), 15.

4. Gordan Wenham, *Genesis 1–15*, Word Biblical Commentary (Zondervan Academic, 2017), 35.

5. See Ezek. 18:23 and 2 Pet. 3:9.

6. This is repeated throughout Scripture. See, e.g., Exod. 34:6; Num. 14:18; Neh. 9:17; Pss. 86:15; 103:8; 145:8; Joel 2:13; Jon. 4:2; Nah. 1:3.

7. John Drane, *The McDonaldization of the Church: Consumer Culture and the Church's Future* (Smyth & Helwys, 2002).

8. C. Christopher Smith and John Pattison, *Slow Church: Cultivating Community in the Patient Way of Jesus* (InterVarsity, 2014).

9. Kent Annan, *Slow Kingdom Coming: Practices for Doing Justice, Loving Mercy and Walking Humbly in the World* (InterVarsity, 2016).

10. John Mark Comer, *The Ruthless Elimination of Hurry: How to Stay Emotionally Healthy and Spiritually Alive in the Chaos of the Modern World* (Random House, 2019); Alan Fadling, *An Unhurried Life: Following Jesus' Rhythms of Work and Rest* (InterVarsity, 2013); and Alan Fadling, *A Year of Slowing Down: Daily Devotions for Unhurried Living* (InterVarsity, 2022).

11. Marva Dawn and Eugene Peterson, *The Unnecessary Pastor: Rediscovering the Call* (Eerdmans, 1999), 15.

12. Eugene Peterson, *The Contemplative Pastor: Returning to the Art of Spiritual Direction* (Eerdmans, 1993), 17.

13. H. Scott Holland, "The Slowness of Mission Work," *The Church Eclectic* 23, no. 23 (1896): 147.

14. Tony Horsfall, *Working from a Place of Rest: Jesus and the Key to Sustaining Ministry* (Bible Reading Fellowship, 2010), 9–11.

15. Alice Fryling, *Too Busy? Saying No Without Guilt* (InterVarsity, 2002), 16–17. Gratitude for this text being referenced in Mark Noll, *Jesus Christ and the Life of the Mind* (Eerdmans, 2013), 62.

16. Michael Harper, *A Faith Fulfilled: Why Are Christians Across Great Britain Embracing Orthodoxy?* (Conciliar, 1999).

17. John Goldingay, *Remembering Ann* (Piquant, 2011).

18. Goldingay, *Remembering Ann*, 23.

19. Goldingay, *Remembering Ann*, 23.

20. Peterson's paraphrase of Matt. 11:29 in The Message.

21. For more on this, see Richard Osslund, "*Imputatio Iustitiae Christi, Liberum Arbitrium in Renatis*, and *Tertius Usus Legis* in Melanchthon's Later Loci" (PhD diss., Concordia Seminary, 1986), chap. 5.

22. Dallas Willard, *Called into Business: God's Way of Loving People Through Business and the Professions* (Willard Family Trust, 2018), 11.

23. This phenomenon has also been called "positive income shock."

24. On the three stages of love, see John Gottman, *Principia Amoris: The New Science of Love* (Taylor & Francis, 2014).

25. Kosuke Koyama, *Three Mile an Hour God* (Orbis, 1979).

Chapter 2 Embrace the Theological Journey

1. See Stanley Grenz and Roger Olson, "Everyone Is a Theologian," chap. 1 in *Who Needs Theology? An Invitation to the Study of God* (IVP Academic, 1996); and Jen Wilkin and J. T. English, *You Are a Theologian* (B&H, 2023).

2. Alister McGrath, *Christian Theology: An Introduction* (Wiley, 2016), 86.

3. See Phil. 2:10 and Acts 4:12 on the distinctive connection of Christian worship and thought to the specific name and person of Jesus.

4. The Message's paraphrase of 1 Cor. 4:5 perfectly captures the spirit of the text: "So don't get ahead of the Master and jump to conclusions with your judgments before all the evidence is in. When he comes, he will bring out in the open and place in evidence all kinds of things we never even dreamed of—inner motives and purposes and prayers."

5. The italicized words in the quoted biblical texts above are intended to draw the reader's attention to the directional aspirations of some people's theology—of getting "ahead" and "beyond" what Christ calls.

6. Roger Olson, *Reformed and Always Reforming: The Postconservative Approach to Evangelical Theology*, Acadia Studies in Bible and Theology (Baker, 2007), 8.

7. Richard Hughes, *How Christian Faith Can Sustain the Life of the Mind* (Eerdmans, 2001), 39.

8. Robert Farrar Capon, *Kingdom, Grace, Judgment: Paradox, Outrage, and Vindication in the Parables of Jesus* (Eerdmans, 2002), 140–44.

9. Christopher West, *Theology of the Body for Beginners: A Basic Introduction to Pope John Paul II's Sexual Revolution* (Ascension, 2004), 21.

10. D. A. Carson writes, "When Peter makes his confession at Caesarea Philippi he has to be told the Father had revealed this to him. . . . Apparently, revelation can take place without the individual knowing it takes place." Carson, *Showing the Spirit: A Theological Exposition of 1 Corinthians 12–14* (Baker, 1987), 162.

11. See A. J. Swoboda, *After Doubt: How to Question Your Faith Without Losing It* (Brazos, 2020), chap. 2.

12. Anselm, *Proslogion*, quoted in Frederick Copleston, *A History of Philosophy* (Image, 1962), 2:177.

13. Augustine, *On the Holy Trinity* 1.3.5, in *A Select Library of Nicene and Post-Nicene Fathers of the Christian Church*, 1st series, ed. Philip Schaff, 14 vols. (Christian Literature, 1886–89; repr., Hendrickson, 1994), 3:19.

14. John W. de Gruchy, "John de Gruchy," in *Letters to a Young Theologian*, ed. Henco van der Westhuizen (Fortress, 2022), 231.

15. Eugene Peterson, *Answering God: The Psalms as Tools for Prayer* (HarperSanFrancisco, 1991), 42–43.

16. Kosuke Koyama, *Three Mile an Hour God* (Orbis, 1979), 7.

17. John Calvin, *Ezekiel I (Chapters 1–12)* (Eerdmans, 1994), 57.

18. Miroslav Volf and Matthew Croasmun, *For the Life of the World: Theology That Makes a Difference* (Brazos, 2019), 131–32.

Chapter 3 Think Slowly

1. *Tractate Eruvin* 53b.

2. See, e.g., A. J. Swoboda, *Subversive Sabbath: The Surprising Power of Rest in a Nonstop World* (Brazos, 2018).

3. Heather Thompson Day (@HeatherTDay), "I had a student once who entered college," X, May 8, 2019, https://x.com/HeatherTDay/status/1126117460858503169. This tweet went viral, with over sixty thousand retweets at one point, but the account no longer exists.

4. For an introduction to cognitive load, see Jan L. Plass, Roxana Moreno, Roland Brünken, eds., *Cognitive Load Theory* (Cambridge University Press, 2010).

5. For more on this, see "Ask the Expert: Do I Have to Be 40 to Study the Kabbalah?," My Jewish Learning, accessed February 3, 2025, https://www.myjewish learning.com/article/ask-the-expert-do-i-have-to-be-40-to-study-kabbalah.

6. Mark Thibodeaux, *God's Voice Within: The Ignatian Way to Discover God's Will* (Loyola, 2010), 36.

7. Kosuke Koyama, "'Not by Bread Alone . . .' How Does Jesus Free and Unite Us?," *The Ecumenical Review* 27, no. 3 (July 1975): 201, 203.

8. Jesse Singal, *The Quick Fix: Why Fad Psychology Can't Cure Our Social Ills* (Farrar, Straus & Giroux, 2021).

9. Ziming Liu, quoted in Nicholas Carr, *The Shallows: How the Internet Is Changing the Way We Think, Read and Remember* (Norton, 2011), 138.

10. Robert Muthiah, *The Sabbath Experiment: Spiritual Formation for Living in a Non-Stop World* (Cascade, 2015), 34.

11. Exod. 3:18; Prov. 4:11, 18; Isa. 43:16.

12. Mark 6:8 and John 14:4–6.

13. Much of this section has been informed by a helpful little section in Jack Hayford, *Living the Spirit-Formed Life* (Regal Books, 2001), 151–53.

14. With gratitude for a reference to this in Ronald Rolheiser, *Against an Infinite Horizon: The Finger of God in Our Everyday Lives* (Crossroad, 2002), 228–29.

15. Gary Moon, *Becoming Dallas Willard: The Formation of a Philosopher, Teacher, and Christ Follower* (InterVarsity, 2018), 44.

Chapter 4 Ponder the Mysteries

1. Douglas Muzzio, "When Boz Came to Town," *City Journal* (Autumn 2018), https://www.city-journal.org/article/when-boz-came-to-town.

2. The theme of David Moffitt, "It Is Not Finished: Jesus' Perpetual Atoning Work as the Heavenly High Priest in Hebrews," in *So Great a Salvation: A Dialogue on the Atonement in Hebrews* (Bloomsbury T&T Clark, 2019), 157–75.

3. Richard A. Muller, *Dictionary of Latin and Greek Theological Terms: Drawn Principally from Protestant Scholastic Theology*, 2nd ed. (Baker Academic, 2017), 125.

4. Gregory of Nyssa, *The Life of Moses*, trans. Abraham J. Malherbe and Everett Ferguson, Classics of Western Spirituality (Paulist Press, 1978), 163.

5. John Scotus Eriugena, quoted in Finn Collin, ed., *Danish Yearbook of Philosophy*, vol. 47 (Museum Tusculanum Press, 2015), 111.

6. Wright says, "All Christian language about the future is a set of signposts pointing into a mist." Wright, *Surprised by Hope: Rethinking Heaven, the Resurrection, and the Mission of the Church* (HarperOne, 2014), 132.

7. Karl Barth, quoted in T. J. Gorringe, *Discerning Spirit: A Theology of Revelation* (Trinity Press International, 1990), 6.

8. On this theme in Bonhoeffer, see John Matthews, "Responsible Sharing of the Mystery of Christian Faith: *Disciplina Arcani* in the Life and Theology of

Dietrich Bonhoeffer," in *Reflections on Bonhoeffer: Essays in Honor of F. Burton Nelson*, ed. Geffrey C. Kelly and C. John Weborg (Covenant, 1999).

9. Joel Lawrence, *Bonhoeffer: A Guide for the Perplexed* (Bloomsbury, 2010), 51.

10. Augustine, *Expositions of the Psalms*, vol. 5, *Psalms 99–120*, trans. Maria Boulding, The Works of Saint Augustine III/19 (New City, 2004), 185–86.

11. Robert Farrar Capon, *The Fingerprints of God: Tracking the Divine Suspect Through a History of Images* (Eerdmans, 2000), 10–11.

12. For a helpful discussion of the difference between a secret and a mystery, see Conrad Gempf, *Jesus Asked: What He Wanted to Know* (Zondervan, 2009), 29–31.

13. Thomas Schmidt, *A Scandalous Beauty: The Artistry of God and the Way of the Cross* (Brazos, 2002), 62.

14. Diogenes Allen, *Temptation* (Cowley, 1986), 62–63.

15. Mark Wallace, *Fragments of the Spirit: Nature, Violence, and the Renewal of Creation* (Bloomsbury Academic, 2002), 17.

16. G. K. Chesterton, *The Book of Job* (Palmer & Hayward, 1916), xxii.

17. See Francis Watson, *The Fourfold Gospel: A Theological Reading of the New Testament Portraits of Jesus* (Baker Academic, 2016).

18. Quoted in Matthias Smalbrugge, "The Presence of the Absent: Augustine and Deification," in *Conversion and Church: The Challenge of Ecclesial Renewal*, ed. Stephan van Erp and Karim Schelkens (Brill, 2016), 31.

19. A paraphrase of the Latin "Si comprehendis, non est Deus" from Augustine, *Sermons* 117.3.5.

20. Michael Welker, *God the Spirit*, trans. John F. Hoffmeyer (Fortress, 1994), 232.

21. Henri Nouwen, *Reaching Out: The Three Movements of the Spiritual Life* (HarperCollins, 1976), 74.

Chapter 5 Go to the Problems

1. Gerhard von Rad, "The Theological Problem of the Old Testament Doctrine of Creation," in *The Problem of the Hexateuch and Other Essays*, ed. Bernard Anderson, trans. E. W. Trueman Dicken (Fortress, 1984), 53–64.

2. Michael V. Fox, *Proverbs 10–31: A New Translation with Introduction and Commentary* (Yale University Press, 2009), 734–35.

3. The work of Wade Mullen has been astoundingly eye-opening in helping us think about "impression management." See, e.g., Wade Mullen, "Impression Management Strategies Used by Evangelical Organizations in the Wake of an Image-Threatening Event" (PhD diss., Capital Seminary, Lancaster Bible College, 2018).

4. Dr. Seuss, *I Can Read with My Eyes Shut* (Beginner Books, 1978).

5. Kevin J. Vanhoozer, introduction to *Dictionary for Theological Interpretation of the Bible*, ed. Kevin Vanhoozer (Baker Academic, 2005), 1:24.

6. Augustine, *On Christian Doctrine* 1.22.21, 1.2.27, 1.35.39.

7. Augustine, *On Christian Doctrine* 1.36.40, 1.36.41, 1.39.43.

8. "Prayer of Saint Richard of Chichester," Loyola Press, accessed February 3, 2025, https://www.loyolapress.com/catholic-resources/prayer/traditional-catholic-prayers/saints-prayers/day-by-day-prayer-of-saint-richard-of-chichester.

9. Richard Hays, "Salvation by Trust? Reading the Bible Faithfully," *Christian Century*, February 26, 1997, 218–23.

10. Hays, "Salvation by Trust?"

11. Hays, "Salvation by Trust?"

12. Augustine, *On Christian Doctrine* 3.15.23.

13. Karen Kilby, "Balthasar and Karl Rahner," in *The Cambridge Companion to Hans Urs von Balthasar*, ed. Edward Oakes and David Moss (Cambridge University Press, 2004), 265.

Chapter 6 Let Pain Be the Altar

1. Alvin Toffler, *Future Shock* (Random House, 1970), 450.

2. Toffler, *Future Shock*, 450.

3. Ronald Rolheiser, *Against an Infinite Horizon: The Finger of God in Our Everyday Lives* (Crossroad, 2002), 100.

4. Toffler, *Future Shock*, 450–51.

5. Stephen Marche, "Is Facebook Making Us Lonely?," *The Atlantic*, April 2, 2012, https://www.theatlantic.com/magazine/archive/2012/05/is-facebook-making -us-lonely/308930.

6. Kate Fagan, "Split Image," *ESPN*, May 7, 2015, http://www.espn.com/espn /feature/story/_/id/12833146/instagram-account-university-pennsylvania-runner -showed-only-part-story. Thanks to Jay Kim for pointing out this heartbreaking story in *Analog Christian: Cultivating Contentment, Resilience, and Wisdom in the Digital Age* (InterVarsity, 2022).

7. Peter J. Williams (@DrPJWilliams), "Fast information is to the brain," X, September 24, 2024, https://x.com/DrPJWilliams/status/1838665913622790245.

8. John Gottman and Julie Gottman, *Fight Right: How Successful Couples Turn Conflict into Connection* (Penguin, 2024).

9. Gordon Fee and Douglas Stuart, *How to Read the Bible for All Its Worth* (Zondervan, 2003), 194.

10. Mark Vroegop, *Dark Clouds, Deep Mercy: Discovering the Grace of Lament* (Crossway, 2019), 26.

11. Marshall McLuhan, *Understanding Media: The Extension of Man* (Routledge & Kegan Paul, 1975).

12. Eugene Peterson, *Answering God: The Psalms as Tools for Prayer* (Harper-SanFrancisco, 1991), 60.

Chapter 7 Believe Together

1. "Dwight Peterson," The Work of the People, accessed February 3, 2025, https://www.theworkofthepeople.com/person/dwight-peterson.

2. Though dated, one of the finest historical and philosophical explorations of this notion is discussed in Nancey Murphy and William McClendon, "Distinguishing Modern and Postmodern Philosophies," *Modern Theology* 5, no. 3 (1989): 191–214.

3. James K. A. Smith, *Desiring the Kingdom: Worship, Worldview, and Cultural Formation* (Baker Academic, 2009), 41.

4. Other translations, such as the RSV, translate this as "common salvation."

5. Dave Davies, "Trees Talk to Each Other. 'Mother Tree' Ecologist Hears Lessons for People, Too," NPR, May 4, 2021, https://www.npr.org/sections/health -shots/2021/05/04/993430007/trees-talk-to-each-other-mother-tree-ecologist-hears -lessons-for-people-too.

6. Quoted in Catherine of Siena, *Saint Catherine of Siena as Seen in Her Letters* (Dutton, 1905), 181.

7. Karl Barth, *Church Dogmatics* I/1 (T&T Clark, 1975), 3.

8. Only twice, both in Matt. 16.

9. Paul even twice sneaks in this word in Acts 19:39–40 to speak of a gathering of a "legal assembly" in the ancient city of Ephesus. An English reader would not necessarily recognize it as the same word, but Paul uses the word *ekklēsia* to describe this legal body. For a helpful overview of the Greek concept of *ekklēsia*, see Robert Banks, *Paul's Idea of Community: Spirit and Culture in Early House Churches*, 3rd ed. (Baker Academic, 2020).

10. Pope Francis, *Evangelii Gaudium* (Catholic Truth Society, 2013), par. 230.

11. This is explored in depth in a fabulous piece by Patricia Killen, "The Religious Geography of the Pacific Northwest," *Word & World* 24, no. 3 (2004): 269–78.

12. Samuel G. Parkison, "The Regulative Principle and the Corporate Recitation of Creeds," *Credo*, January 11, 2023, https://credomag.com/2023/01/the-regulative -principle-and-the-corporate-recitation-of-creeds.

13. Luke Timothy Johnson, *The Creed: What Christians Believe and Why It Matters* (Doubleday, 2003), 7.

14. Johnson, *The Creed*, 40–41.

15. Ben Myers, *The Apostles' Creed: A Guide to the Ancient Catechism* (Lexham, 2018), 12.

16. Myers, *Apostles' Creed*, 12.

17. Thomas Jefferson, letter to Timothy Pickering, February 27, 1821, https:// founders.archives.gov/documents/Jefferson/03-16-02-0548 (slightly revised for clarity).

Chapter 8 Don't Ever Give Up

1. Dietrich Bonhoeffer, *The Cost of Discipleship* (SCM, 2015), 91.

2. Eugene Peterson, *A Long Obedience in the Same Direction: Discipleship in an Instant Society* (InterVarsity, 2019).

3. Sean Ingle, "The Self-Transcendence 3100 Mile Race: A Long Distance Love Affair," Coach, May 31, 2016, https://www.coachweb.com/running/5419/the-self -transcendence-3100-mile-race-a-long-distance-love-affair.

4. Brad Stulberg and Steve Magness, "How Extended Breaks in Training Help Elite Athletes—and Why You Should Take Them Too," *Sports Illustrated*, June 7, 2017, https://www.si.com/edge/2017/06/07/peak-performance-book-extended -breaks-rest-workouts.

5. The consequences of which are fleshed out in E. Randolph Richards and Richard James, *Misreading Scripture Through Individualist Eyes: Patronage, Honor, and Shame in the Biblical World* (InterVarsity, 2020).

6. Henri Nouwen, *Adam: God's Beloved* (Orbis, 1997), 24.

Conclusion

1. Alfred Tennyson, "In Memoriam A. H. H. OBIIT MDCCCXXXIII: 96," available at https://www.poetryfoundation.org/poems/45349/in-memoriam-a-h-h-obiit -mdcccxxxiii-96.

A. J. SWOBODA

(PhD, University of Birmingham) is assistant professor of Bible, theology, and world Christianity at Bushnell University. He also leads a doctor of ministry program around Christian formation and soul care at Friends University. He is the author of over a dozen books, including the award-winning *Subversive Sabbath* and *After Doubt*. With Nijay, he cohosts the *Slow Theology* podcast. He is married to Quinn and is the proud father of Elliot. They live and work in Eugene, Oregon.

Connect with A. J.

🌐 www.ajswoboda.com

f theajswoboda

📷 @a.j.swoboda

✖ @mrajswoboda

📑 ajswoboda.substack.com

NIJAY K. GUPTA

(PhD, Durham University) is Julius R. Mantey Professor of New Testament at Northern Seminary. He is cohost of the *Slow Theology* podcast, founder of the popular *Engaging Scripture* (Substack), and author of numerous books, including *Tell Her Story, A Beginner's Guide to New Testament Studies, 15 New Testament Words of Life, Strange Religion,* and commentaries on Galatians, Philippians, Colossians, and 1 and 2 Thessalonians. He is also a senior translator for the New Living Translation. Gupta lives in Portland, Oregon.

Connect with Nijay

nijaykgupta.substack.com

nijay.gupta

@nijay.gupta

@nijay.gupta